W9-BYZ-645

Jesus, the Bible,
and Homosexuality

Jesus, the Bible, and Homosexuality

Explode the Myths, Heal the Church

JACK ROGERS

WESTMINSTER
JOHN KNOX PRESS
LOUISVILLE • KENTUCKY

© 2006 Jack Rogers

All rights reserved. No part of this book may be reproduced or transmitted in any form or by any means, electronic or mechanical, including photocopying, recording, or by any information storage or retrieval system, without permission in writing from the publisher. For information, address Westminster John Knox Press, 100 Witherspoon Street, Louisville, Kentucky 40202-1396.

Scripture quotations from the New Revised Standard Version of the Bible are copyright © 1989 by the Division of Christian Education of the National Council of the Churches of Christ in the U.S.A. and are used by permission.

Book design by Drew Stevens
Cover design by Eric Walljasper, Minneapolis, MN

First edition
Published by Westminster John Knox Press
Louisville, Kentucky

This book is printed on acid-free paper that meets the American National Standards Institute Z39.48 standard. ⊗

PRINTED IN THE UNITED STATES OF AMERICA

06 07 08 09 10 11 12 13 14 15 — 10 9 8 7 6 5 4

Library of Congress Cataloging-in-Publication Data is on file at the Library of Congress, Washington, D.C.

ISBN-13: 978-0-664-22939-9

ISBN-10: 0-664-22939-5

To my son, Toby Rogers
—with whom it is a privilege to work

Contents

Preface

Why am I doing this? I am not gay. No one in my family is gay. That is why I was able to stay on the sidelines for so long. It didn't touch me personally.

I am a Christian who cares deeply about Christ's church. The church is being torn apart by controversy over whether people who are homosexual can have full rights of membership.[1] Not just my own Presbyterian Church, but all of the denominations in this nation are divided.

Our country is also being rent by this controversy. Attitudes toward people who are lesbian, gay, bisexual, and transgender—LGBT—are among the factors that have divided us into red and blue states, rural versus urban areas, midlands versus the coasts. How we choose to respond to this issue is a test of who we will become as a nation.

This is a defining issue of our time. For some it is an issue of maintaining traditions and customs that have given order to our society. For others, it is an issue of justice—all citizens should be entitled to equal rights under the law. For me, it is a moral and spiritual issue. How can the church live up to the highest ideals of Jesus Christ? How can we most faithfully act according to the central principles of the Bible? How can we most honestly and equitably share the love of God with all people?

I first dealt with this issue in the local congregation where my wife, Sharon, and I worship. Since that time I have explored it using my training as a scholar. I have not specialized as a biblical scholar, but I have wrestled with the biblical texts that are most commonly cited regarding people who are homosexual. I have not specialized as a church historian, but I have delved deeply into the history of how we have coped with other bitterly divisive issues in the church. I am a theologian and a historian of doctrine (the beliefs of the church), especially in its creeds and confessions. Seeking guidance from the church's central traditions, I have looked afresh at these foundational documents of the church.

I am a minister and a teacher, and I had the honor to be elected the Moderator of the 213th General Assembly of the Presbyterian Church

(U.S.A.) in 2001. The Moderator is sort of an honorary head of the church for one year.[2] I had the privilege, as Moderator, of traveling all over the United States, and in several foreign countries. I met people in congregations with 15 members and congregations with 4,500 members.

I have been exposed to every kind of opinion on the issue of whether LGBT people should have equal rights in the church and in society. I have encountered people red-faced with anger who have shouted at me. I have met people who wept because they felt rejected. I have met people who just didn't want to be involved in controversy. I have known people who could not quite understand what the fuss was all about. I have come to know a great many people who are homosexual that I am now grateful to call my friends.

I want the church to be healed of this great wound in the body of Christ. My favorite seminary professor often said: "If Christ is divided, who bleeds?"[3] My attitude toward this problem has changed. For a long time I thought that we just had to wait, that time would heal the controversy. I no longer believe that. The Presbyterian Church took that attitude toward slavery until the nation and the church were finally torn in two.

I have gone through a change in my mind and heart. I have gone from being a silent spectator to actively working for change. I believe people who are homosexual should be given full rights of membership in the church and citizenship in the nation. I believe that this is the only way to heal the wounds of the church and the nation.

We in the church are not living according to the ideals of our Savior and Sovereign, Jesus Christ, when we discriminate unjustly against any group of people in our midst. To act unjustly weakens our witness to Christ in the world. I believe that we will be one holy and whole church only when all our members are treated equally. Then, together we will be able to evangelize, worship, and serve with the integrity of those who live according to Christ's teachings. To help us reach that goal is my reason for writing this book. I invite all who share the goal of healing the church to join me as I describe my journey of discovery and my change of mind and heart.

In this book each chapter represents a step in my own journey. In chapter 1, "Studying Homosexuality for the First Time," I describe how my journey began, on a task force in my local congregation to study the status of people who are lesbian or gay. Then I wanted to know how the church had dealt with other, similarly volatile, issues. In chapter 2, "A Pattern of Misusing the Bible to Justify Oppression," I review how our leading theologians, for two hundred years, preached and taught that the Bible justified the enslavement of people of African descent and the subordination of women to men.[4] In chapter 3, "A Breakthrough in Understanding the Word of God," I present the dramatic change in biblical interpretation that began in the 1930s, and rejoice in the way that it supported movements toward equality for African Americans and liberation of women from limiting stereotypes. Chapter 4, "Interpreting the Bible in Times of Controversy," tells the story of how, in the 1980s, the Presbyterian denominations, north and south, developed guidelines for biblical interpretation. Here I walk through seven guidelines, see their support in our Reformed confessions, and consider their application to the lives of people who are gay and lesbian. In chapter 5, "What the Bible Says and Doesn't Say about Homosexuality," I study in detail the usual biblical texts that are cited to condemn homosexual behavior and the theories, imposed on these texts, that twist their meaning. Chapter 6, "Real People and Real Marriage," will enable us to move beyond stereotypes by introducing us to the powerful witness of faithful gay and lesbian Christian couples. In chapter 7, "Recommendations for the Presbyterian Church (U.S.A.)," I look back on what we have learned and discuss the appropriate action that will move us forward. In that chapter I make recommendations for what the Presbyterian Church can do to right the wrongs of our present situation and to heal the divisions in the church. I hope that people in other denominations facing these same issues will be encouraged to reflect on the parallels in their setting and plan what they will do to bring healing to their communities.

Let us begin.

Acknowledgments

I have dedicated this book to my son, Toby Rogers, himself a writer, who has been deeply invested in this project from its inception. He helped to shape and focus the stories and the argument of the entire work.

My wife, Dr. Sharon Rogers, along with her significant work in special education, for forty-eight years has always made time to encourage and support me, and for that I am grateful.

Stephanie Egnotovich, my editor with Westminster John Knox Press for the past ten years, has been patient with my delays and gracious in continuing to encourage me. I value her friendship and especially appreciate her support for this project from its beginning and through all of its various incarnations. I was helped additionally by the comments of WJK editor and friend Don McKim.

The Huntington Library in San Marino, California, has provided me with the most helpful research and writing environment possible: an office with a door; access to an incomparable collection of historical and literary works which enabled me to research the history of institutional change regarding race, women, divorce, and now homosexuality; and beautiful gardens in which to lunch and chat and walk with other scholars.

Dean Thompson was very gracious to let me tell a part of his story while I was telling mine. I thank the many people who generously read and critiqued an earlier version of this study. Many of their insights are now imbedded in the text. Where I failed to profit from their insights, the fault is mine. Thanks go to Scott Anderson, Pam Byers, Gary Demarest, Bob Lodwick, Bill Pannell, Bear Ride, Mel White, and John Wilkinson. I am especially grateful for the continuing conversations with my Huntington lunch and walking partners, Ron White and Paul Zall, and to Henk van de Rest for providing an international perspective. Others who read a later version and commented helpfully include Bill Hopper, Ron Oglesbee, Mark Smutny, and Susan Hylen on chapter 5.

I have benefited by the opportunity afforded by the Covenant Network of Presbyterians to present portions of this study at their national and regional conferences. I have learned from the interaction with students in my classes at San Francisco Theological Seminary, Southern California, and from people in numerous congregations where this material has been discussed.

I am well aware that some will challenge my conclusions. I acknowledge that controversy on the subject of homosexuality may continue for some time. My earnest hope is that, as with the conflicts over race, women, and divorce, the church will finally admit all of its members to the full rights of membership and discover in doing so that we all will benefit and the church will be healed.

Jack Rogers
September 28, 2005

1

Studying Homosexuality for the First Time

Dean Thompson was faced with a problem.

As pastor and head of staff at the Pasadena Presbyterian Church, Dean (as he was affectionately known by his congregation) was confronted with an issue that he would rather have avoided. In the spring of 1993, a gay man, who had earlier been elected a deacon, wrote to the session,[1] the local governing body, of the Pasadena Presbyterian Church. He asked the session to initiate a program of study and, at the end of a year, formally consider designating Pasadena Presbyterian Church a More Light Church—a congregation that was willing to ordain gay, lesbian, bisexual, and transgender people to all offices in the church, despite a denominational prohibition against it.[2] The gay man's action was supported by the deacons and a number of elders.[3] Consequently, the session asked the three pastors on the staff to establish a task force to create an educational program that would sensitize the whole congregation to gay and lesbian issues.

Dean had grown up in West Virginia and earned both an MDiv and a PhD in American church history from Union Seminary in Richmond, Virginia. He served pastorates in West Virginia and in Austin, Texas, before accepting the call to Pasadena Presbyterian Church in California. A genial and humble person, he was known for loving his congregation and for preaching biblical sermons, grounded in the Reformed tradition.

Pasadena Presbyterian Church was older than the city itself. It had a history of great preachers. It had been a leading voice in the community during the civil rights struggle.

Now Dean was in a no-win position. If the task force recommended in favor of becoming a More Light Church, several more traditional families would surely leave the church. If the task force recommended against becoming a More Light Church, members who supported equal rights for people who are gay and lesbian, including openly gay members and their families, would feel alienated and possibly leave. To his credit, Dean assembled a diverse task force that included a broad representation of different people and viewpoints.

Dean knew that I was opposed to the ordination of gay and lesbian people. He asked me to be a member of the task force.

I said no.

I thought I had a perfect excuse. Although I worshipped regularly at Pasadena Presbyterian Church, as an ordained Presbyterian minister, my membership was not in the local congregation, but in the presbytery, the regional denominational governing body.

Then Dean put his request on a personal level: "If you are my friend, you will do this." I probably had many reasons for resistance, but they all came down to my not wanting to be involved in studying the issue of ordaining gay and lesbian people to church office. It just was not a problem that I wanted to take on. Reluctantly, I acceded to Dean's request and agreed to serve.

The three pastors on the church staff appointed a task force of fifteen members who, among them, covered the whole range of opinions. It included the gay man who had requested the task force and the mother of a lesbian young woman who had grown up in the congregation. One more conservative couple on the task force left the church when we began to look at more than what they considered the only biblical perspective. A retired missionary also on the task force said he would stand in the church door to bar a lesbian evangelist, Janie Spahr, from entering the building.

After nearly a year of study, the task force presented a twelve-week adult education course at Pasadena Presbyterian Church. More than one hundred people attended each class meeting. We devoted three sessions to biblical interpretation and three to psychological and sociological perspectives. We heard from gay and lesbian members of the West Hollywood Presbyterian Church and looked at videos on different responses by family members. We spent one session discussing what was in the best interests of children. We listened to people who said that sexual orientation or behavior could be changed. We studied the denomination's form of government to see how it affected this issue. And we designed the final session with two opposing speakers again to balance the viewpoints. We tried very hard to be balanced and fair to every perspective, but invariably some thought we had not given their view enough support.

As an educator, I thought the curriculum was excellent, but the results of the study were mixed. The congregation as a whole did seem more comfortable with the issue.[4] The session did not vote to become a More Light Church. The gay man who had initiated the process was disappointed and left the church. And for the first time in my career, I had been forced to study the issue.

During this period I did not change my Reformed theology or my method of biblical interpretation. For the first time, however, I had to apply them to the issue of homosexuality. That has led me on a journey that in many ways has been uncomfortable. In other ways it has resulted in growth and satisfaction. I want to share that journey with you. I hope it will encourage you in your own journey.

MY FORMATION AS AN AMERICAN
EVANGELICAL CHRISTIAN

Let me begin by putting my own life experience in context. In 1934 my devout, Christian parents had a healthy, white, male baby. In Nebraska, at the state fair each year, there was a judging, not only of pigs and calves, of apple pies and bread-and-butter pickles, but of children. My parents entered me in a contest. I don't know what the criteria were, but I do have a silver trophy inscribed "1935, NEBR STATE FAIR, MOST PERFECT BOY." When I looked at that trophy many years later, it was a visible confirmation for me of what most white, American males experienced. We knew that in some intangible but very real way we were superior. As I grew older and became aware of an attraction to girls, I subconsciously added another element to my personal list of male superiority. I was heterosexual.

The culture of the 1940s and 1950s reinforced that stereotype of superiority. The jokes, the ways teachers related to us, the opportunities we were given made us know that boys were better than girls, that whites were better than coloreds, and that straights were normal and queers were not.

It took the civil rights movement of the 1960s to begin to crack the facade of white racial superiority. In the 1970s, the women's movement forced a grudging acknowledgment that women were of equal value to men. In the late 1980s and the 1990s, the first awakenings began to come for many people that gay and lesbian people were different in some respects, but of no less worth than people who were heterosexual.

During all of this time I was also an evangelical. I was baptized a Methodist. I became a Presbyterian by geography, after my father was drafted into the Navy in World War II and we were forced to sell our car. There was a small neighborhood United Presbyterian church just a block and a half from our house. We began to attend there and continued after the war. I grew up in that church until I left home to attend seminary.[5]

The old United Presbyterian Church of North America (UPCNA) was a small denomination (about 250,000 members). It was conservative, but not fundamentalist.[6]

The pastor under whom I joined the church was named Harold (Shorty) Irwin. I was about twelve years old and was impressed that, as a former cheerleader, he could walk on his hands. He also made us study and memorize large sections of the Bible. Those of us in his communicants class understood that we were lost in sin and that Christ had paid the penalty for our sins and that by trust in Christ we received our salvation. I believed it then, and I believe it now. As I grew older, I also sometimes attended the local Youth for Christ meetings. I went "down the aisle" several times confirming my sense of being saved.

That small church gave me many opportunities for leadership. I was the president of our presbytery youth organization. I also had the opportunity to attend several national youth conferences. My first was at Lake Geneva, Wisconsin. There I met attractive young people and capable pastors who encouraged me in my Christian growth. One summer I won the national Bible reading contest. The speakers at these conferences were often professors from our one denominational seminary, Pittsburgh-Xenia. I was drawn to their message, as I was drawn to them personally.

Those national youth conference experiences were a significant factor in my feeling called to the ministry as a sophomore in college. During Christmas break I counseled with my pastor about my sense of vocation. His advice was, "Don't go into the ministry if you can be happy doing anything else." That did it. I decided that I couldn't be happy doing anything else. The most dramatic moment for me came one evening when, after praying, I got up off my knees, walked into my parents' bedroom, and announced that God had called me into the ministry. The conviction of that calling has never left me.

Given my background, it was natural for me to head to Pittsburgh-Xenia Seminary when I graduated from the University of Nebraska. I knew that I was a conservative Christian. At seminary, I learned that in the larger Christian culture we were called evangelical.

At seminary I learned a particular Anglo-Saxon, American, Presbyterian tradition that was presented as Christian orthodoxy. This orthodoxy was defined confessionally by the Westminster Confession of Faith, and the Westminster Confession was interpreted theologically in the tradition of Charles Hodge and Benjamin B. Warfield of nineteenth-century Princeton Seminary.[7] Practically, orthodoxy was defined as the most adequate understanding of life and reality. Our task was to defend it reasonably and to preach it using interesting illustrations and practical applications.

My view of orthodoxy was that it had come down in an unbroken line from the apostle Paul to Augustine to Calvin to the Westminster Confession to Warfield and then to my professors of theology and church history. I believed that all of them were treating Scripture in the same way. I always felt that the key to the Christian life and a better world was understanding and interpreting Scripture. The doctrine of Scripture was always my chief academic interest.

When I graduated from seminary, I wanted to go on to study for a doctorate in theology, and I had the good fortune to receive a modest scholarship for one year of study overseas. One of my seminary professors, John Gerstner, urged me instead to go to Harvard, as he had, where I would be confronted with liberal theology and become stronger by fighting against it. That didn't appeal to me. I wanted a deeper understanding of the Reformed tradition.[8] I consulted with Cary Weisiger, the senior pastor of a large church where I was interning. He suggested I study with G. C. Berkouwer at the Free University of Amsterdam in the Netherlands. Dr. Weisiger felt that Professor Berkouwer was deeply Reformed and also fair in his assessments of others. Berkouwer was engaged in writing a series of volumes on the main topics of theology. That sounded like just what I wanted.

I identified with Abraham! One of my favorite verses in Scripture is, "And he set out, not knowing where he was going" (Heb. 11:8). Since my wife and I were going overseas, I requested ordination by my presbytery on the grounds that if I had an opportunity to serve while I was in the Netherlands, I couldn't come running back to Nebraska. So they ordained me as a traveling evangelist!

Four years in the Netherlands were transformative in our lives. I did my course work and comprehensive examinations. In our second year, my wife, Sharon, got a job teaching school for English-speaking children of Dupont engineers in Dordrecht. I became the organizing pastor of an English-speaking congregation for the Dutch Reformed Church, serving the same English-speaking community. Our first son, Matthew, was born. Then we moved to New Wilmington, Pennsylvania, so I could teach at Westminster College (one of the six UPCNA colleges).

After two years there, I took an unpaid leave of absence to finish my dissertation. Sharon and Matthew and I spent the summer in Princeton, where I made use of the Speer and Firestone libraries. Then we flew to London for six months of research at the British Museum Library. I took twelve metal boxes, each with a thousand quote cards, back to Holland, where I could work with my doctoral professor. After another ten months of writing, I graduated in January of 1967 with a printed dissertation entitled *Scripture in the Westminster Confession* and returned to teaching at Westminster College.[9]

TEACHING AT FULLER THEOLOGICAL SEMINARY

Four years later, I received a call to teach philosophy of religion at Fuller Theological Seminary, a multidenominational, evangelical seminary in Pasadena, California. I was then engaged in translating and editing G. C. Berkouwer's two-volume work on *Holy Scripture*, so in my first quarter at Fuller I gave a seminar on Berkouwer's doctrine of Scripture.[10] My memory is that four students signed up. We had a good time and I was continuing to pursue my longtime interest in interpretation of the Bible.

As a professor of philosophical theology at Fuller I was immersed in the culture of the evangelical world. The struggle to develop an evangelicalism distinct from its formation in fundamentalism was played out at Fuller Seminary.[11] In the late 1940s, Billy Graham, Harold John Okenga, Carl F. H. Henry, and others developed a movement called evangelicalism, which was distinguished from the militant fundamentalism that separated from the mainstream churches and stood against changes in American society.

I would define an evangelical theologically as someone who accepts three propositions: (1) People can and should have a personal relationship with God through trust in Jesus Christ. (2) The Bible is the final authority for salvation and living the Christian life. (3) God's grace in Jesus Christ is such good news that everyone should hear about it. If you add something to these affirmations, you are becoming denominational or fundamentalist. If you take away one of these affirmations, you could still be a Christian, but you would not be an evangelical.

Sociologically, evangelicalism was a movement, not a church. It was a loose coalition of people within the mainstream churches, independent associations of Christians, and parachurch organizations. Fuller Seminary was founded as its intellectual center. *Christianity Today* was its magazine. Billy Graham's revivals were a source of its members.

I am an evangelical theologically and have always been so. I am not, and never have been, completely comfortable in the evangelical subculture. I am distrustful of movements. I prefer established organizations where there are clear lines of responsibility and accountability. I need to be in a congregation that is related to other congregations in a denomination with publicly known processes for handling problems. I believe in representative democracy, where there are clear procedures and checks and balances so that the majority may move forward while the minority is able to continue to advocate for its view. I am distrustful of self-appointed leaders and of informal organizations, held together by commitment to charismatic individuals. I want equitable processes for dealing with disputes, rather than some individual guru acting as arbitrator.

Too often the media lump together evangelicals and fundamentalists—leaving the general public confused as to the distinctions between these two groups. Within evangelicalism there are a right, left, and middle regarding political and cultural issues.[12] Fundamentalism is more monolithic politically and more conservative theologically than evangelicalism. Fundamentalists like Jerry Falwell know that.[13] But the confusion serves the fundamentalists' purpose by making it appear that they have a larger constituency, and thus influence, than they do.

The doctrine of inerrancy was and is a hallmark of fundamentalism.[14] For some of its proponents, inerrancy is a symbol for the authority of the Bible and simply affirms that the Bible is true. For others, inerrancy is a particular theory about the interpretation of the Bible. Inerrancy holds that the Bible gives accurate and up-to-the-minute information, not only on religious matters, but on all things that the Bible addresses, including science and history. It encourages a literal reading of Scripture.[15]

Shortly before I joined the faculty at Fuller, the faculty had removed a clause in the seminary's statement of faith referring to the Bible as inerrant. The Fuller faculty preferred to use the word "infallibility," which had historically been used in the church to mean that the Bible accomplishes its purpose of bringing people to a saving knowledge of God and guiding them in living the Christian life.

This theological change evoked an attack on the Fuller Seminary by its former vice president, Harold Lindsell, in a book entitled *The Battle for the Bible*.[16] My evangelical credentials were apparently strong enough for President David Hubbard to ask me to edit a volume in reply to Lindsell and to write the historical chapter in it; that book was *Biblical Authority*.[17] I asked my friend and former student Don McKim to assist me in preparing the historical chapter, with the promise that later he and I would publish a major book on this topic. Following my yearlong sabbatical in 1977–78, the book that Don and I coauthored appeared in 1979 as *The Authority and Interpretation of the Bible: An Historical Approach*.[18] It engendered a cottage industry of books by people intent on retaining and rehabilitating the concept of inerrancy as the only acceptable descriptor of the Bible.[19]

Fundamentalists and those on the far right of evangelicalism were not happy with me.[20] However, Fuller Seminary was the leading institution at the center of evangelicalism, and I was a fully acceptable representative of that centrist evangelicalism. I was frequently called upon to speak at evangelical churches and conferences.

Upon returning to Fuller after my sabbatical in 1978, I discovered that many of our Presbyterian students were being pressured by their presbytery committees on preparation for ministry to transfer to a Presbyterian seminary. In response, with administration support, I created an Office of Presbyterian Ministries and became its director. We created four courses in Presbyterian distinctives and a Monday morning meeting for Presbyterian students, and I acted as liaison between the seminary and the presbyteries. I interpreted Fuller Seminary to the Presbyterians, and I interpreted the Presbyterians to Fuller Seminary.

President Hubbard supported my efforts to bring about a better relationship with the Presbyterian Church. While at Fuller I had the good fortune to serve on three national committees of the denomination, including the Task Force on Biblical Authority and Interpretation that met from 1978 to 1982 and produced official guidelines for interpreting Scripture in times of controversy. In all of these endeavors I felt privileged to be working on the issue that I cared most about, biblical interpretation. I felt a harmony between my role as a theological evangelical and my position as a Reformed theologian in the Presbyterian Church. Either as a member of a denominational committee or at the behest of Fuller Seminary, I attended the General Assembly of the Presbyterian Church almost every year.

THE CHURCH DEBATES BIBLICAL
INTERPRETATION AND HOMOSEXUALITY

In 1976, the issue of the ordination of people who are homosexual was first broached at the United Presbyterian Church in the U.S.A. (UPCUSA) General Assembly in Baltimore.[21] I was there and followed discussions in committee and the debates in plenary session. The Presbytery of New York City asked the assembly for what is called "definitive guidance," an official counsel on whether a candidate for the ministry, who was in all other respects well prepared for ministry, could be ordained if that person was a "self-affirming, practicing homosexual." The assembly responded by creating a Task Force to Study Homosexuality.

I was also present in 1978 when the task force reported. The 1978 assembly in San Diego, California, was rich with discussion of biblical interpretation. The Task Force to Study Homosexuality had submitted a 201-page study document including majority and minority recommendations.[22] It included data from psychotherapy and the empirical sciences. What captured the attention of most members of the assembly, however, was a 70-page section entitled "Homosexuality and the Bible: A Re-examination." A subsection on "How to Read the Bible? Problems and Models of Biblical Authority and Interpretation" evoked the most comment, because, for the first time in decades, Presbyterians had in hand four alternative approaches to biblical interpretation. Each was supported with theological assumptions, cited authorities, and suggested applications.

The report labeled the four models A, B, C, and D; each model had a rough correlation with an identifiable theological school of thought. Model A was the scholastic theology of the Old Princeton School of Charles and A. A. Hodge and B. B. Warfield that dominated the northern Presbyterian Church from 1812 to 1927. Model B could be likened to the neo-orthodoxy of the 1930s through the 1960s, citing Karl Barth, Emil Brunner, Dietrich Bonhoeffer, and the Confession of 1967. Model C was a form of liberation theology, supported by Gordon Kaufman, Dorothee Soelle, Paul Lehmann, and Rosemary Radford Ruether, among others. Model D continued the liberation motif but added the emphases of process theology represented by Norman Pittenger, John Cobb, David Ray Griffin, and Daniel Day Williams.[23]

Model A proposed that ordination of people who are homosexual be forbidden on grounds of the law of God. Model B came to the same conclusion but attributed it to the Spirit of Christ. Model C argued that ordination of people who are homosexual should be permitted on the basis of justice. Model D supported that view and added love as a further reason.

The Task Force majority of fourteen people found the biblical and theological grounds in Models C and D adequate to advocate for the ordination of qualified gay and lesbian people. A five-person minority reported that homosexual behavior was sinful and that ordination should be denied on grounds given in Models A and B. The minority argued that a homosexual orientation was not sinful in itself and that gay and lesbian people could therefore be members of the church, but sexually active people who are homosexual could not be ordained to office, because the "practice" of homosexuality was sinful.[24]

The assembly chose, not the majority report, but the minority report of the Task Force to Study Homosexuality. At the same time, it endorsed civil rights for people who are homosexual. The assembly's pronouncement was in the form of "definitive guidance," counsel, rather than law. It acknowledged that for ministers of Word and Sacrament, ordination was the province of the presbytery, not the national church.[25]

An additional reason for the sensitivity of the assembly is that Presbyterians are the only Protestant denomination for whom the rules of government that apply to ministers of Word and Sacrament apply to deacons and elders as well. All three groups of ordained officers must answer affirmatively the same eight ordination questions.[26] Then each group takes one additional vow that applies to its specific function—service for deacons, governance for elders, and preaching, teaching, pastoral care, and governance for ministers of Word and Sacrament. Thus Presbyterian denominational rules that prohibit people who are homosexual from being ordained to church office apply more generally than rules in some other Protestant denominations, where only ministers are affected.

Studying Biblical Authority and Interpretation

A second report that came to the 1978 UPCUSA Assembly further focused attention on Scripture. In 1976 a Committee on Pluralism had been created to study sources of conflict in the church. The report concluded:

> Of all the factors that contribute to divisiveness in our denomination, the Committee found none is more pervasive or fundamental

than the question of how the Scriptures are to be interpreted. In other words, the widely differing views on the ways the Old and New Testaments are accepted, interpreted, and applied were repeatedly cited to us by lay people, clergy, and theologians as the most prevalent cause of conflict in our denomination today. . . . It is our opinion that until our church examines this problem, our denomination will continue to be impeded in its mission and ministry, or we will spiral into a destructive schism.[27]

(This last statement proved to be predictive. Between 1979 and 1981 approximately sixty churches left the UPCUSA. Most of these churches claimed a "higher view" of biblical authority as their reason for leaving.)

The confluence of these two reports, on homosexuality and on Scripture, which demonstrated great diversity in biblical interpretation within the United Presbyterian Church in the U.S.A. (the northern stream), caused the assembly to set up a Task Force on Biblical Authority and Interpretation in 1978. I was privileged to be appointed a member of the task force, which reported to the UPCUSA in 1982.

The most important mandate of the task force was to present "recommended guidelines for a positive and not a restrictive use of Scripture in theological controversies."[28] A subcommittee of the task force carefully studied the UPCUSA *Book of Confessions* that contains eleven theological documents, from the Nicene Creed to confessions of the Protestant Reformation to three twentieth-century theological statements. From these sources the subcommittee derived six guidelines for interpreting Scripture. When our report came to the General Assembly, the committee of delegates assigned to this report developed an appropriate seventh guideline. As you will see, I use these guidelines in chapter 4 of this book.

In 1979, the Presbyterian Church in the United States (PCUS, the southern stream of the Presbyterian church) set up a parallel study on "The Understanding and Use of the Bible in the Presbyterian Church in the United States."[29] The resulting 1983 PCUS report incorporated the seven UPCUSA guidelines but reorganized and expanded them into nine. Using extensive citations from the *Book of Confessions*, the report documented the sources of the guidelines. This report, "Presbyterian Understanding and Use of Holy Scripture," proved to be a helpful study document that was in harmony with the guidelines adopted by the UPCUSA in 1982.

In identifying guidelines for interpreting Scripture, both northern and southern denominations had anticipated the reunion in 1983. Their task forces on the Bible exchanged papers, sent visitors to one another's meetings, and produced reports that were intentionally in harmony. The two reports were later published in one booklet.[30]

The Developing Debate on Homosexuality

In 1993 gays and lesbians at the General Assembly pushed for greater recognition and acceptance. At one point, some thirty gay and lesbian people were given the opportunity to come to a microphone on the stage and state simply, "My name is _____. I am gay (or lesbian). I want to offer my service to the church." It appeared later that this peaceful and respectful demonstration influenced enough commission-ers to prevent passage of a motion that would have put a prohibition against homosexual ordination into the *Book of Order*, thus making it church law. Instead, the assembly asked the church to study the matter for three years. The Evangelical Lutheran Church in America, the United Church of Christ, and the United Methodist Church all attempted similar study processes in the 1990s.[31]

Concerned with the apparent growing acceptance of gays and les-bians, some conservatives pushed back. A group of pastors of large, theo-logically conservative churches met and formed an organization that later grew into an umbrella group called The Coalition.[32] Its first pub-lic action was a letter, prepared at the General Assembly in Orlando, dated June 8, 1993. In the letter the group noted that it regretted the request to study the issue of the ordination of homosexuals but noted that the three-year study period could be an occasion to speak with "conviction and clarity" in support of the traditional position of the church. I joined nearly 200 Presbyterian members, elders, deacons, missionaries, and ministers in signing the letter.

By 1996, less than 3 percent of Presbyterian congregations reported having engaged in a congregational study of the issue.[33] My experience suggests that the reason for this extremely low percentage is that many people think there is nothing to study, while others just feel uncom-fortable talking about sex. The culture of most Americans, including church people, has taught them that homosexuality is sin. They feel no need to investigate further. Indeed, one highly placed Presbyterian offi-cial said in my presence, "My grandma told me it was wrong and that's good enough for me."[34]

From 1993 to 1996 the Presbyterian Church made no effort to mount any official denominational study, and as a result there were no new official documents to which people might respond. Writers both progressive and conservative attempted to fill that vacuum. Pressure for a decision regarding the ordination of people who are homosexual began to build as the period of study was coming to an end. The 1996 Presbyterian General Assembly in Albuquerque received fifty-one overtures (proposals for legislative action) relating to the ordination to church office of gay and lesbian people.

New scholarly work often appears in response to changes in the ecclesiastical or cultural scene. Writing and publishing books takes a long time. In 1996, only a half dozen books by recognized scholars were available. Two of them, collections of essays by Presbyterian seminary faculty, *Biblical Ethics and Homosexuality: Listening to Scripture*, ed. Robert L. Brawley (Louisville, KY: Westminster John Knox, 1996), and *Homosexuality and Christian Community*, ed. Choon-Leong Seow (Louisville, KY: Westminster John Knox, 1996), were not published until just before the July 1996 assembly and thus had little influence on its decisions.

Since 1996, there has been a steady flow of new works, both in support of and opposed to ordination of people who are homosexual. Scholars representing a wide range of church backgrounds are probing for new approaches to interpreting the biblical tradition. These are live issues for scholars in the Episcopal Church, United Church of Christ, United Methodist Church, Evangelical Lutheran Church in America, American Baptist Church, and Roman Catholic Church, to name only some of those whose work I cite in this book.

In 1996, the Presbyterian Church (U.S.A.) tightened its prohibition on ordaining gay and lesbian people to church office by putting the prohibition into its *Book of Order*, thus taking it from "definitive guidance" to church law. The statement reads:

> Those who are called to office in the church are to lead a life in obedience to Scripture and in conformity to the historic confessional standards of the church. Among these standards is the requirement to live either in fidelity within the covenant of marriage between a man and a woman . . . or chastity in singleness. Persons refusing to repent of any self-acknowledged practice which the confessions call sin shall not be ordained and/or installed as deacons, elders, or ministers of the Word and Sacrament.[35]

Other denominations have enacted similar prohibitions in words that reflect their polity and tradition. The debate over homosexuality crosses all religious lines and is of critical interest in American culture.

It is not going away anytime soon. We need to be as informed as possible in order to cope constructively with what affects all of us.

AN ISSUE FOR ALL OF US

I want to share with you some of what I have learned through studying this issue. I will naturally speak from my own context as a Presbyterian. But, the issue of accepting lesbian, gay, bisexual, and transgender people as fully human and equal to other people in the eyes of God is not exclusively a Presbyterian issue. By 1991, more than one hundred statements on homosexuality had been published by forty-seven denominations and religious organizations.[36]

Because of our different forms of church government, the focus of concern may differ among denominations. For Presbyterians, the issue comes to focus in the question of ordination to church office as deacons, elders, or ministers of Word and Sacrament. For Episcopalians, the issue doesn't become critical until someone is elected a bishop. That emotional chasm was crossed for Episcopalians with the consecration of an openly gay man, the Rev. Gene Robinson, as a bishop in November 2003. For some Southern Baptists, the issue is avoidance of any appearance of approval, through ordination, employment, or granting civil benefits, to people who are homosexual. In every case, however, we are debating the fate of faithful Christian people who are members of our churches.

These church contexts have parallels in our social and political life as a nation. Now, in the first decade of the new century, debate over the issue of same-sex marriage has moved to center stage in politics and the public mind. On July 1, 2000, Vermont became the first state legally to recognize civil unions between same-sex couples. On June 26, 2003, the United States Supreme Court, in *Lawrence v. Texas*, overturned a Texas law that had criminalized sodomy for homosexuals only.[37] On November 28, 2003, the Massachusetts Supreme Judicial Court ruled that same-sex couples had a legal right to marry under the Massachusetts Constitution.[38]

Less than two months later, on January 20, 2004, President George W. Bush, in his State of the Union address, declared that the nation must "defend the sanctity of marriage."[39] On February 12, 2004, San Francisco mayor Gavin Newsome authorized city clerks to grant marriage licenses to same-sex couples. Following that, on February 24, 2004, President Bush called on Congress to pass an amendment to the federal Constitution defining marriage as between one man and one woman.[40] Republicans in Congress made such an amendment a top legislative priority.

In the elections in November 2004, voters in eleven states approved referenda defining marriage as between a man and a woman. Legislating who can be married, or who has the right to care for children, go to the hospital with a loved one, or enter into civil contracts as a couple, impacts all of us. Every American is aware of the issue of marriage between people of the same sex, and most recognize that we are all affected in some way by the struggle between maintaining the status quo and moving in a new direction.

Some fear that any change in attitude toward people who are homosexual would mean the end of Western civilization as we know it.[41] For example, James Dobson, of Focus on the Family, exclaims, "Barring a miracle, the family as it has been known for more than five millennia will crumble, presaging the fall of Western civilization itself."[42] For others, a new openness to LGBT people would fulfill our commitment as a nation to liberty and justice for all. Extending equal rights to people who are homosexual is a critical issue for our time. How we deal with it will determine, to a large degree, the kind of people, church, and nation we will become. This book is intended as a contribution to that important discussion.

How My Mind Changed

I have had a change of mind and heart. I had never really studied the issue of the status in the church of people who are homosexual. I opposed homosexuality reflexively—it was just what I thought Christians were supposed to do. However, studying this issue in depth for the first time brought me to a new understanding of the biblical texts and of God's will for our church. The process was both very serious and painful. I wasn't swayed by the culture or pressured by academic colleagues. I changed my mind initially by going back to the Bible and taking seriously its central message for our lives.

Since then, my new conviction has been reinforced from many sources. I have studied how the church changed its mind on other moral issues. I worked through how the church, guided by the Holy Spirit in understanding the Scriptures, reversed our prohibitions against ordination to leadership for African Americans, women, and divorced and remarried people. I saw a clear picture of a shift from a literalistic method of biblical interpretation to one that looks at Scripture through the lens of the redeeming life and ministry of Jesus Christ. I studied the principles of biblical interpretation found in our Reformed confessions and discovered a continuity through history to our best practices today. I have wrestled with the biblical texts usually cited in this discussion and come to a new understanding of them. I came to know many gay and lesbian people and have had my Christian life enriched by their profound witness to the gospel. I now know many people across all theological and ideological lines who are convinced that the Spirit of Christ is leading us, based on our best understanding of the Bible, to be consistent in allowing all of our baptized members eligibility for positions of leadership.[43] My desire is to reframe the discussion regarding people who are homosexual so that we can better understand one another, heal our divisions, and move forward together in our churches.

I did not arrive at my conclusions overnight. I do not expect you to do so, either. If you, as was the case for me, have not given this issue much attention, I hope this can be the occasion for you to investigate it more fully. If you feel sure that people who are homosexual, including Christians, should not have equal rights in the church and society, I urge you to walk with me through these chapters and at least to give yourself permission to consider what I am reporting, rather than to reject it before you begin. Jesus said to his disciples: "If you continue in my word, you are truly my disciples; and you will know the truth, and the truth will make you free" (John 8:31–32). Those disciples had to change their minds a lot of times as they learned from Jesus. I had to as well.

2

A Pattern of Misusing the Bible to Justify Oppression

Homosexuality is not the first social issue with which the Presbyterian Church has wrestled that invokes high emotion. There have been many issues that, at the time, seemed to threaten the unity, indeed the very existence, of the church. Sabbath observance was one. Prohibition was another. In 1926 the Presbyterian Church in the United States of America General Assembly debated whether people using tobacco could be ordained to the Gospel ministry.[1]

Surely the most important social issues in the American experience to which the churches have responded are slavery/segregation and the role of women. Another potentially instructive issue, which I will take up in the next chapter, is the question of divorce and remarriage of Christian people. On each of these issues, at one point the church had near unanimity of opinion and then, over time and painfully, changed its mind to almost the exact opposite view. What can we learn from how the church dealt with these issues in the past?

Many people who are opposed to full rights of membership for people who are homosexual ignore these historical analogies. Others immediately assert that the condition of being black or female is quite different from what they consider to be willful behavior like "homosexual practice." These people read Scripture regarding slavery and women as manifesting both a diversity of views and as evidencing hints toward the position that the church now takes. At the same time, they read Scripture as uniformly and unremittingly negative regarding any form of homosexual practice.[2]

All of these arguments miss the point. The issue is not what we *now* think about slavery and women. The issue is, What did American Christians think about these subjects for more than 200 years when the accepted view was completely different than what we now think? What did Christians believe about these issues when they believed what almost everyone in the general culture believed? How could most Christians for more than 200 years accept slavery and the subordination of women with not a hint that there was any other view in the Bible? Why did good, intelligent, devout Christian people not see what we now recognize as mitigating factors in the biblical record? Why did we change our minds? How did we change our minds? How does a church change its course? Potentially, at least, we can learn something relevant to our discussion of homosexuality by discovering the answers to these questions.

I used a sabbatical leave to study how the Presbyterian Church, north and south, had dealt with slavery/segregation and the role of women. To my amazement, the same pattern appeared in each case. What was that pattern? In each case, we accepted a pervasive societal prejudice and read it back into Scripture. We took certain Scriptures out of their context and claimed to read them literally with tragic consequences for those to whom these verses were applied.

Let us begin with the ugly history of slavery and segregation and the way the Bible was used to justify such oppression. For more than 200 years, most Americans, including Christians, shared three assumptions regarding slavery and segregation. Most people believed that (1) the Bible records God's judgment against the sin of people of African descent from their first mention in Scripture; (2) people of African descent were inferior in moral character and incapable of rising to the level of full white, "Christian civilization"; and (3) people of African descent were willfully sinful, often sexually promiscuous and threatening, and they deserved punishment for their own acts.[3] We abhor such views now, but most Christians considered such views "natural" and "common sense" in the past. Let us look at the evidence.

HOW THE BIBLE WAS USED TO JUSTIFY SLAVERY

The Curse on Ham and Canaan

Genesis 9:20–26 was the key text used to justify slavery:

> And Noah began to be a husbandman, and he planted a vineyard: And he drank of the wine, and was drunken; and he was

uncovered within his tent. And Ham, the father of Canaan, saw the nakedness of his father, and told his two brethren without. . . . And Noah awoke from his wine, and knew what his younger son had done unto him. And he said, Cursed be Canaan; a servant of servants shall he be unto his brethren. And he said, Blessed be the LORD God of Shem; and Canaan shall be his servant.[4]

Although it is nowhere stated in the biblical text that Ham is the ancestor of the black race, the Western theological tradition so designated him. The curse placed on Ham was used as the justification for slavery. Since his son Canaan was mentioned, it was further assumed that the curse continued beyond Ham and was justly applied to all of Ham's supposedly dark-skinned descendants.

Since Ham's exact sin is not specified in the text, the interpretation of this text from the Jewish rabbis down through the ancient and medieval church and into nineteenth-century America incorporated many of the evils that human beings attribute to those who are a feared "Other." The hint of sexual misconduct always lurked in the background.

Augustine in the *City of God* provided a formulation that virtually became church doctrine. Augustine argued that slavery was justified because of the sin of the person enslaved: "It is with justice, we believe, that the condition of slavery is the result of sin. And this is why we do not find the word 'slave' in any part of Scripture until righteous Noah branded the sin of his son with this name. It is a name, therefore, introduced by sin and not by nature."[5]

Stephen R. Haynes in his book *Noah's Curse* documents the application of Genesis 9:20–26 to the justification of slavery, the attribution of sexual sin, and the assignment of dark skin to Ham and his descendants from the Jewish rabbis, through the early church theologians, medieval Christendom, the Reformation, the early modern period, the Enlightenment, down into the nineteenth century.[6] I will therefore focus on these arguments as they were applied to defend American enslavement of Africans.

Prior to and, for some, even after the Civil War, the leading theologians of the Presbyterian Church were absolutely confident that Africans were cursed and deserved slavery both for their nature and their willful sin. These theologians were not evil people per se. They were among the best thinkers and church leaders of their day. The church wholeheartedly agreed with them.

James Henley Thornwell

James Henley Thornwell (1812–62) was just such a theologian. Thornwell was a pastor, a college president, and from 1855 until his death at age fifty the professor of didactic and polemical theology at Columbia Theological Seminary. He was also actively involved in the church. As a commissioner (delegate) to the Old School Presbyterian General Assembly in 1845, Thornwell wrote to his wife, "I have no doubts but that the Assembly, by a very large majority, will declare slavery not to be sinful, will assert that it is sanctioned by the word of God, that it is purely a civil relation with which the Church, as such, has no right to interfere, and that abolitionism is essentially wicked, disorganizing, and ruinous."[7]

In an 1850 sermon Thornwell painted a clear picture that Christians supported slavery and atheists opposed it: "The parties in this conflict are not merely Abolitionists and Slaveholders; they are Atheists, Socialists, Communists, Red Republicans, Jacobins on the one side, and the friends of order and regulated freedom on the other. In one word, the world is the battleground—Christianity and atheism the combatants; and the progress of humanity the stake."[8]

When Presbyterians in the South separated from their northern counterparts in 1861, it was Thornwell who was asked to write a manifesto to the world justifying their actions. The resulting seventeen-page pamphlet was presented and adopted unanimously by the Presbyterian Church in the Confederate States of America, which met in Augusta, Georgia, on December 4, 1861.

In this manifesto, Thornwell used literalism in interpreting the Bible to justify slavery, and according to which, as we shall see, particular verses of Scripture take precedence over general principles, in contradiction of Reformed principles of biblical interpretation.

Thornwell began by identifying a set of significant cultural assumptions concerning the ordering of society: Man's "most solemn earthly interests, [are] his country and his race."[9] He also assumed that a class system was natural, biblical, and essential, writing, "If men had drawn their conclusions upon this subject only from the Bible, it would no more have entered into any human head to denounce slavery as a sin, than to denounce monarchy, aristocracy or poverty."[10]

According to Thornwell, human rights were subordinated to a hierarchical class system instituted by God. He assumed that Africans were descendants of Ham, by nature inferior to whites, and therefore assigned by God to the status of slaves. That status was deemed, therefore, in the slaves' best interest, for God assigned each person a place in the hierarchy according to that person's competency to fulfill his/her duties. Referring to a slave, Thornwell asserted, "There are no doubt, many rights which belong to other men . . . to his master, for example—which are denied to him. But is he fit to possess them? The truth is, the education of the human race for liberty and virtue, is a vast Providential scheme, and God assigns to every man, by a wise and holy decree, the precise place he is to occupy in the great moral school of humanity."[11]

As Thornwell saw it, slavery was a good, necessary, and normal condition for Africans in America. "As long as that race, in its comparative degradation, co-exists, side by side, with the white, bondage is its normal condition. . . . Indeed, as we contemplate their condition in the Southern States, and contrast it with that of their fathers before them, and that of their brethren in the present day in their native land, we cannot but accept it as a gracious Providence that they have been brought in such numbers to our shores, and redeemed from the bondage of barbarism and sin."[12]

Thornwell next asked, "Is slavery, then a sin?" and began to lay the groundwork for his reply: "In answering this question, as a Church, let it be distinctly borne in mind that the only rule of judgment is the written word of God."[13] For Thornwell, the written word of God and his nineteenth-century "common sense" always agreed.

Thornwell then put two questions. First, do the Scriptures directly condemn slavery? His answer was no! "Slavery is no new thing. . . . It has not only existed for ages in the world, but it has existed, under every dispensation of the covenant of grace, in the Church of God."[14]

Second, do the Scriptures indirectly condemn slavery? Again his answer was no! He acknowledged the requirements of love and justice, writing, "Let us concede, for a moment, that the laws of love, and the condemnation of tyranny and oppression, seem logically to involve, as a result, the condemnation of slavery." But then he clarified the method of his newly articulated theory: "Yet, if slavery is afterwards expressly mentioned and treated as a lawful relation, it obviously follows, unless Scripture is to be interpreted as inconsistent with itself, that slavery is, by necessary implication, excepted."[15] An evil practice of ancient Near Eastern culture, recorded in the Bible, was thus allowed to overrule central teachings of Jesus.

Thornwell developed a form of biblical interpretation according to which the particulars of Scripture take precedence over the general principles: Unless something is expressly prohibited, it can be done.

Nothing ought to be done unless there is a specific biblical warrant for it. Thus the presence or absence of particular verses took precedence over general principles, including the gospel of Christ.

From this hermeneutic, or method of interpretation, grew Thornwell's doctrine of the "spirituality of the church," which became a central principle of southern Presbyterianism for almost a century and was used to justify both slavery and segregation. Southern Presbyterians, following Thornwell, claimed that the Bible affirmed both slavery and segregation. Furthermore, they believed that the church should not be involved in dealing with such secular social problems. Judgments about both slavery and segregation were to be left to the conscience of individuals and regulation by the state.

Thornwell also offered a natural-law argument—what his common sense accepted he assumed to have the divine character of a natural law: "Whatever is universal is natural. We are willing that slavery should be tried by this standard."[16] Confidently he went on, "But what if the overwhelming majority of mankind have approved it? What if philosophers and statesmen have justified it, and the laws of all nations acknowledged it."[17] On that argument, that all people recognized a law of nature justifying slavery, Thornwell rested his case.

Shortly before his death in 1862, Thornwell wrote to his wife, "Every day increases my sense of the value of the principles for which we are contending. If we fail, the hopes of the human race are put back for more than a century."[18] The human race, for Thornwell, was structured hierarchically. For him, the well-being of the "inferior classes," such as Africans, depended on the power and benevolence of the ruling classes, which in this case meant southern white men.

Robert Lewis Dabney

Robert Lewis Dabney was the premier theologian of the southern Presbyterian Church from 1865 until 1892. He became the chief public voice of the Presbyterian Church in the South after Thornwell's death. Dabney was a professor at Union Theological Seminary in Virginia. In 1861, Dabney had enlisted in the Confederate Army, where he served first as a chaplain and then as a major on the staff of a personal friend, General Thomas (Stonewall) Jackson.[19]

While the war was still in progress, Dabney published the first volume of *A Defense of Virginia*, which contained a one-hundred-page defense of slavery based on his interpretation of the Bible. The second volume followed in 1867. Dabney's views remained, if anything, stronger following the South's defeat.

In his two volumes, Dabney set forth a genetic argument for the inferiority of Africans, arguing that blacks and whites were different and unequal species. That implied for him that blacks were less capable than whites in most aspects of life: "But while we believe that 'God made of one blood all nations of men to dwell under the whole heavens,' we know that the African has become, according to a well-known law of natural history, by the manifold influences of the ages, a different, fixed *species* of the race, separated from the white man by traits, bodily, mental and moral almost as rigid and permanent as those of *genus*."[20]

Granting social equality to blacks, according to Dabney, was unthinkable. He believed that the North's goal was to dilute the "pure racial heritage" of the South by promoting intermarriage of blacks and whites: "Hence the offspring of an amalgamation must be a hybrid race, stamped with all the feebleness of the hybrid. And this apparently is the destiny which our conquerors have in view. If indeed they can mix the blood of the heroes of Manassas with this vile stream from the fens of Africa."[21]

Dabney brought a sexual component into the picture by alluding to "the indecent and unnatural sin of Ham." Although he did not specify what that sin might be, he did view slavery as God's "punishment of and remedy for . . . the peculiar moral degradation of a part of the race."[22]

After the Civil War, some prominent white southern pastors argued for the full equality of African Americans in the church, including ordination to the ministry. In 1867, some Presbyterian pastors in Virginia chose a moment when Dabney was absent from a meeting of the Synod to propose: "Resolved . . . that ordination to the work of the Gospel ministry is to be given to all those called of God to and qualified for that work without respect of persons."[23]

Action on the motion was delayed, and the next day Dabney was given the opportunity to speak. He saw the situation in apocalyptic terms, calling it "a moment of life and death for the church."[24] He argued passionately against ordination to the ministry for African Americans: "Every hope of the existence of Church, and of State, and, of civilization itself, hangs upon our arduous effort to defeat the doctrine of negro suffrage."[25]

Dabney appealed to the deep-seated fears of his white male audience: "He must be 'innocent' indeed, who does not see whither all this tends, as it is designed by our oppressors to terminate. It is (shall I pronounce the abhorred word?) to *amalgamation!*"[26] Dabney raised the specter that if African Americans were ordained it might mean "this Negro of yours, reviewing and censuring the records of white sessions, and sitting to judge appeals brought before you by white parties, possibly by white ladies!"[27] He continued to press the possibility of a physical mixing of the races. "Do you tell me that after you have admitted this Negro thus to your debates, your votes, your pulpits, your sick and dying beds, your weddings and funerals, you will still exclude him from your parlours and tables? . . . I tell you, Sir, this doctrine, if it does not mean nothing, or if it does not mean Yankee hypocrisy, means ultimately, *amalgamation.*"[28]

Dabney's speech made it clear that he was not simply reacting to the consequences of American slavery. Rather, he was proclaiming a doctrine of white racial superiority. He argued his point by appealing to what he viewed as the racial inferiority of Mexicans compared to their pure-blooded Castilian conquerors: "We have before our eyes in Mexico, the proof and illustration of the satanic wisdom of their [Yankee] plan. There we saw a splendid colonial empire, first blighted by abolition; then a frantic spirit of leveling, declaring the equality of the coloured races with the Spaniard; and last, the mixture of the Castilian blood—the grandest of all the Gothic—resulting in the mongrel rabble which is now the shame and plague of that wretched land."[29]

The motion to open ordination to all who were called of God and qualified for the work was defeated. With his speech, Dabney turned southern Presbyterian attitudes away from the possibility of racial integration to developing a system of segregated institutions for persons of color.[30]

In 1888, twenty-three years after emancipation, Dabney was still using these arguments. In an article entitled "Anti-Biblical Theories of Rights" he defended slavery. Dabney announced, "The radical social theory asserts, 'all men are born free and equal.'"[31] Dabney contended, "The honest student, then, of the New Testament can make nothing less of its teachings on this point than that domestic slavery, as defined in God's word and practiced in the manner enjoined in the Epistles, is still a lawful relation under the new dispensation as well as the old."[32]

Dabney then grounded his argument in the ancient story of Ham and Canaan: "In Genesis ix. 25–27, Ham the son of Noah, is guilty of an unfilial crime. His posterity are condemned with him and share the penalty to this day. In Ex. Xx. 5, God declares that he will visit the iniquity of the fathers upon the children to the third and fourth generations."[33]

For Dabney, and the southern church, the bottom-line reason for the enslavement of people of African descent was the belief that their foreparents willfully chose to sin—and that this sinful condition and its penalties were passed on to their posterity for all time. Dabney believed that African Americans, as a "degraded race," continued to behave sinfully in the present.

To Dabney, racial purity was the ultimate value, and racial segregation was essential to protect the purity of the white race. The loss of the Civil War had already meant the loss of "the honor, the hospitality, the integrity, everything which constituted Southern character." What had to be maintained at all cost was the superiority of the white race, exemplified in the "ruling class" of white Southerners.[34]

The same arguments used to justify slavery were also used to justify the subordination of women to men.

HOW THE BIBLE WAS USED TO OPPRESS WOMEN

In the previous section, we saw vivid illustrations of how leading Christian theologians applied three nonbiblical assumptions to people of African descent. These same assumptions were also applied, by men, to women for more than 200 years. Men argued that (1) the Bible records God's judgment against the sin of women from their first mention in Scripture (the curse on Eve); (2) women were inferior in moral character and incapable of rising to the level of full white, male Christian civilization (because women were seen as emotional and not rational); and (3) women were willfully sinful, often sexually promiscuous and threatening, and deserved punishment for their own acts (women tempt men).[35]

The Curse on Eve

The biblical text used to support this distorted view of women is in Genesis 3:1–16 (selected verses):

> 1 Now the serpent was more subtle than any beast of the field which the LORD God had made. And he said unto the woman, Yea, hath God said, Ye shall not eat of every tree of the garden? . . . 6 And when the woman saw that the tree *was* . . . pleasant to the eyes, and

a tree to be desired to make *one* wise, she took of the fruit thereof, and did eat, and gave also unto her husband with her; and he did eat. . . . [13] And the LORD God said unto the woman, What *is* this *that* thou hast done? And the woman said, The serpent beguiled me, and I did eat. . . . [16] Unto the woman he [God] said, I will greatly multiply thy sorrow and thy conception; in sorrow thou shalt bring forth children; and thy desire *shall be* to thy husband, and he shall rule over thee. (KJV, 1611)

The early church theologian Tertullian in the third century identified Eve as the origin of sin in a manner that has been repeated endlessly: *"You* are the Devil's gateway. *You* are the unsealer of that forbidden tree. *You* are the first deserter of the divine Law. *You* are she who persuaded him whom the Devil was not valiant enough to attack. *You* destroyed so easily God's image of man. On account of *your* desert, that is death, even the Son of God had to die."[36]

Traditional Christian culture had long portrayed woman as a sexual temptress. She was thought to have little control over her primal sexual urges. Men were constantly warned to avoid women lest they be seduced and brought down by them.[37]

In the nineteenth century, women were spoken of more gently but nonetheless kept carefully segregated from any place of power. America was shifting from an agrarian to an industrial society. As men left farms for factories, the role of women changed. Now they were not colaborers in the fields, but were given a separate sphere from men, the home, with care of children the foremost priority. In the Victorian era in America, as Betty DeBerg notes, "a relatively quick turn-around was accomplished . . . when women were transformed from sensual temptresses to 'passive partners with little sexual appetite.'"[38] The argument still was that men were rational and women were emotional and therefore unfit for positions of leadership in the public sphere.

Even after the formation in 1789 of the first Presbyterian General Assembly in America, two decades passed before women were even mentioned in the official documents of the Presbyterian Church. The first recognition came for their work in voluntary organizations for missions, benevolence, and reform. In 1811 the General Assembly made its first formal acknowledgment of the positive role of women in the church: "It has pleased God to excite pious women to combine in association for the purpose of aiding, by their voluntary contribution (to the church). . . . Benevolence is always attractive, but when dressed in female form possesses peculiar charms. . . . We hope the spirit which has animated the worthy women of whom we speak will spread [to] animate other bosoms."[39] In that same year, a Presbyterian minister, Matthew La Rue Perrine, supported the concept of women joining together in their own organizations, but in a typically patronizing manner: "Who will not delight in the sweet and heavenly work of honouring the weaker vessels, and of endeavouring to make them ornamental and useful in the house of God?"[40]

Ornamental Womanhood

From 1825 to 1855, three leading theologians of the Old School Presbyterian Church attempted to counsel pastors and church members on the role of women. Princeton Seminary professors Charles Hodge, Archibald Alexander, and Samuel Miller wrote on "ornamental womanhood" in the *Biblical Repertory and Princeton Review*, advising that women's activities should be limited to piety, sobriety, and righteousness in the wedded and maternal state, and that no female should attempt to assume any authority. The Princeton Association of Gentlemen, including the three noted above, probably got their concept of "ornamental womanhood" from a 1692 treatise of New England minister Cotton Mather, who wrote a manual for women entitled *Ornaments for the Daughters of Zion, of the Character and Happiness of a Vertuous Woman*. "Ornaments" were the essential qualities that should clothe the female character. Women should express their piety in private. The public realm was for men only. The "female sex" was to complement the male role by its radiant but silent presence.[41]

We need especially to note the impact of Charles Hodge (1797–1878), the leading figure among these "gentlemen," and a seminal influence in shaping Presbyterian attitudes toward women. Hodge was on the faculty of Princeton Seminary for fifty-eight years. He trained 3,000 seminarians, more than any other American in the nineteenth century. Every year, with one exception, from 1835 to 1867, Hodge wrote an influential review of the actions of the General Assembly. His three-volume *Systematic Theology*, published in 1872, remained the standard text at Princeton and was used in many American seminaries into the 1930s and some places as late as 1960.[42]

We should not be surprised to discover that Hodge, in company with most men of his day, opposed public education, abolitionism, and women's suffrage. Hodge's attitude toward women centered in his understanding of marriage and family values. As he wrote, "marriage is a divine institution ordained by God for His glory and the happiness of men." While a husband in the marriage ceremony had to promise to be "faithful and loving," the woman had in addition to promise to be "obedient."

Hodge, in a book review, used the analogy of the necessary subordination of women to defend slavery:

> If women are to be emancipated from subjection to the law which God has imposed upon them; . . . if, in studied insult to the authority of God, we are to renounce, in the marriage contract, all claim to obedience, we shall soon have a country over which the genius of Mary Wollstonecraft would delight to preside, but from which all order and all virtue would speedily be banished. . . . there is no deformity of human character from which we turn with deeper loathing than from a woman forgetful of her nature and clamorous for the vocations and rights of men.[43]

There were parallels in the southern Presbyterian Church (PCUS). Theologian Robert L. Dabney of the PCUS in 1888 developed a rationale for denying women leadership in the church. He argued that God's curse on Eve was applicable to women for all time, claiming, "'The woman was first in the transgression,' for which God laid upon Eve two penalties (Gen. iii.16), subordination to her husband and the sorrows peculiar to motherhood. The New Testament declares (I Tim. ii.11 to end) that it is right her daughters shall continue to endure these penalties to the end of the world. (See also I Peter, iii. 1–6.)"[44] Dabney was repeating here the interpretative tradition established by the rabbis and handed down through the ancient and medieval church into nineteenth-century America. At the same time he relied on the general cultural acceptance of the notion that women were cursed by "Eve's transgression." Dabney denounced women's rights, declaring, "Another hostile banner is already unfurled, and has gathered its millions of unbelievers for a new attack on God's Word."[45]

In 1891 the PCUS General Assembly denied women the right to speak, lead in prayer, and participate in public discussions in mixed assemblies. It did however affirm the propriety of women holding meetings among themselves, "for mutual edification and comfort by pious conversation and prayer."[46] The notion that women might organize themselves into larger, for example, presbyterial, groups for service was denounced by PCUS ministers and characterized as "unscriptural, un-

Presbyterian, unwomanly." The declaration caused one PCUS woman to declare that the men could see "the cloven hoof of woman's suffrage under our petticoats."[47]

The PCUS General Assembly in 1916 adopted a resolution that prohibited women to "publicly expound God's Word" from the pulpit or to be ordained or licensed, reaffirming actions taken by previous General Assemblies. However, this 1916 resolution omitted any reference to women's right to speak in "promiscuous assemblies," by which they meant those with men as well as women in attendance, and recommended that "other services of women be left to the discretion of the sessions and the enlightened consciences of our Christian women themselves." Sixty-one commissioners immediately protested that the resolution went too far and might allow women to speak in the local congregation's prayer meeting, which the protestors believed would be a reversal of the position of the PCUS without scriptural warrant. The assembly answered sharply: "The Scriptures may have their authority discredited not merely by a violation of their precepts, but also by any attempt on the part of ecclesiastical courts to bind the consciences of God's people on matters of doubtful interpretation."[48] Thus early in the twentieth century, a PCUS assembly recognized that there was doubt about the correctness of the traditional interpretation of Scripture that limited women's rights in the church. However, most of the church's male ministers continued to maintain the rightness of racial segregation and the suppression of women's rights to full participation in society.

HOW CHURCH AND SOCIETY GOT IT WRONG

How could learned men like Thornwell, Dabney, and Hodge ignore basic principles of the Bible such as love your neighbor as yourself, and do unto others as you would have them do unto you? And why were their theological arguments accepted so uncritically by others? What were the intellectual sources that allowed people to view customs of the ancient Near East as directly applicable to nineteenth-century America? How could certain theologians and pastors be so confident that they understood the Scriptures, when we now believe that they were so wrong? What were the primary philosophical and theological resources of early America that directed people to think in ways that we now can hardly comprehend?

The answers to these questions can be found by examining the influence of Scottish Common Sense philosophy and the Scholastic theology of Francis Turretin.

The dominant theological tradition in nineteenth-century America was fully developed at Princeton Seminary with its founding in 1812 and practiced until the 1940s. Archibald Alexander established the curriculum at Princeton Seminary in 1812. He recommended Scottish Common Sense philosophy as the method of biblical interpretation. He chose as the textbook in theology, not Calvin, nor any of the writers of the Westminster Confession, but the *Loci* (Topics) of the late-seventeenth-century Swiss scholastic Francis Turretin. Let us briefly examine each of these influential intellectual influences in turn.

Scottish Common Sense Philosophy

Common Sense philosophy was developed in Scotland by Thomas Reid (1710–96). It came to the College of New Jersey (which became Princeton University) when the Scot John Witherspoon became president in 1768. It was the pervasive American philosophical view when American colleges and universities were being formed, and so had a greater degree of influence than it might have had in another time or in other circumstances.[49]

According to Scottish Common Sense philosophy, people should accept what was the common sense of all humankind—that we know the reality of the world exactly as it is. Everyone can be a scientist by simple observation of the "facts" of nature. Charles Hodge, as an ardent follower of Common Sense, asserted that "the Bible is to the theologian what nature is to the man of science. It is his storehouse of facts."[50] A word in a book was to Hodge a fact, in just the same way as an object was in nature.

Furthermore, all people, in all places and at all times, think alike, at least those of the "better classes" do. Everyone can know, for example, exactly what the apostle Paul was thinking without any knowledge of ancient languages or cultures. Scottish Common Sense accepted no problems of interpretation. The truth is obvious.[51]

This essentially democratic and egalitarian philosophy fit the American mind-set. Thomas Jefferson in Paris in 1789 met a disciple of Reid's philosophy named Dugald Stewart. Enthralled, he declared Stewart one of the greatest of thinkers. The first words that Jefferson wrote in the Declaration of Independence could have come straight from Scottish Common Sense: "We hold these truths to be *self-evident* [emphasis added]."[52] The truth is obvious.

At age sixteen the bookish and precocious James Henley Thornwell, who would later support slavery by theological argument, had come across a copy of Dugald Stewart's *Elements of the Philosophy of the Human Mind*. Thornwell later said that he "felt that his fortune was now made." His biographer, Benjamin Palmer, called Scottish Common Sense philosophy "the pivot upon which his whole intellectual history subsequently hinged."[53]

Thornwell, as a Common Sense thinker, had what was, for his time, a "modern" method of proving things to be true. He employed two sets of "facts," arguing that we must "accept the facts of revelation as we accept the facts of nature."[54] Both of Thornwell's sets of facts were fit together in a rational system built in large part on the commonsense assumptions of nineteenth-century southern, white, American culture.

This rationalistic and literalistic use of Scripture allowed Thornwell to defend slavery. Since the Bible did not explicitly condemn it, and since it was practiced universally, it could be assumed to be legitimate.[55] Texts could be taken from their ancient Near Eastern cultural setting and used as universal laws in nineteenth-century America.

Francis Turretin

Francis Turretin was professor of theology in Geneva more than one hundred years after Calvin and a decade after the Westminster Confession of Faith was written in England. Turretin's theology provided a framework into which the "facts" of the Bible could be fitted. Charles Hodge declared, "So the Bible contains the truths which the theologian has to collect, authenticate, arrange, and exhibit in their internal relation to one another."[56] Scottish Common Sense philosophy enabled the theologian confidently to understand the "natural" meaning of the "facts" he observed in nature or read in the Bible. Turretin's theology provided the framework in which these "facts" could be properly arranged.

By emphasizing "facts" over faith and using natural law to organize those "facts," Turretin and his followers created a method that allowed social prejudice to receive biblical sanction. If slavery was mentioned in the Bible and if slavery had occurred throughout history, they therefore assumed that slavery must be supported by the Bible and sanctioned by God.

Whatever theory of interpretation people use powerfully affects how they understand Scripture. Common Sense philosophy and Turretin's theology allowed seemingly good, intelligent, devout people to ignore the basic principles and lessons of Scripture and to brutalize other human beings by enslaving them. The combination of Common Sense and Turretin enabled people to use the Bible to claim divine justification for common cultural prejudices.

The theologians at Princeton and their graduates who were spread all over nineteenth-century America had what for them was a method of certain knowledge. Ascertain the "facts" in nature and Scripture by Scottish Common Sense philosophy, and arrange them in Turretin's theological system. Southern theologians adopted the same philosophical and theological methods as their northern counterparts. Many persisted in their antiabolitionist and proslavery views even after the end of the Civil War.

ABOLITIONISM AND THE WHOLE BIBLE

While Thornwell, Dabney, and Hodge confidently proclaimed that the Bible mandated such things as slavery, racial hierarchy, and oppression of women, other groups of Americans read the Bible and came away with a different view. For example, Christian abolitionists saw slavery as a "stain on the character of American Christianity."[57]

Abolitionists appealed to the Bible as a whole, and gave priority to its central themes, especially that Jesus was the central figure in Scripture and that he always displayed love, which required remedying injustice for those who were oppressed.[58] John Rankin, a leading Presbyterian abolitionist, summarized this argument: "The whole Bible is opposed to slavery. The sacred volume is one grand scheme of benevolence. Beams of love and mercy emanate from every page, while the voice of justice denounces the oppressor, and speaks to his awful doom."[59]

Christian abolitionists had been influenced by the Great Awakening, an evangelical revival that swept across the country in the opening decades of the nineteenth century. Individuals were called on to repent of their personal sins and to work for the moral improvement of the community.

Abolitionists were also influenced by postmillennialism, the idea that Christ would return to earth and reign after an ideal, moral society had been established.[60] This idea offered a powerful incentive to Christian abolitionists to rid the world of the unchristian blot on society of African enslavement in America. By working to end slavery, abolitionists were preparing the way for Christ's return to earth.

Enslaved Africans, although not formally educated, knew that the Bible, properly understood, did not sanction oppression. Abolitionists within the larger denominations, following the principle "no fellowship with slavery," often withdrew to form new antislavery churches.[61] Among these were the Wesleyan and Free Methodist churches and several black denominations such as the African Methodist Episcopal and African Methodist Episcopal Zion. Some smaller denominations like the Quakers, the United Brethren, and the Covenanters had been consistently antislavery.

Yet other abolitionists grew tired of the mainstream churches' failure to condemn slavery. For example, a leading New England abolitionist, William Lloyd Garrison, was deeply disappointed when his own pastor, Lyman Beecher, refused to endorse immediate emancipation of the slaves, calling the idea "commendable, but misguided."[62] Garrison and some of his followers reacted by rejecting the authority of the clergy and the divine inspiration of the Bible.[63]

We now know, of course, that the Christian abolitionists got it right. Their method of biblical interpretation looked at the Bible as a whole and gave priority to its central themes, especially that Jesus was the central figure in Scripture and the one we should seek to emulate. Their method of biblical interpretation anticipated the adoption a century later of a Christ-centered method of biblical interpretation by the "Christian mainstream."

CONCLUSION

When we study the church's historical positions on race and the role of women, a clear pattern emerges: In each case, leaders in the church claimed that (1) the Bible records God's judgment against the sin of people of African descent and women from their first mention in Scripture; (2) People of African descent and women were somehow inferior in moral character and incapable of rising to the level of full white male, "Christian civilization"; and (3) people of African descent and women were willfully sinful, often sexually promiscuous and threatening, and deserved punishment for their own acts.

How did they get it so wrong? They followed Scottish Common Sense philosophy and the theology of Francis Turretin, rather than putting their trust in the teachings of Jesus Christ.

What is instructive about these examples is that a similar pattern is emerging today regarding people who are homosexual. Those who oppose homosexuality claim that (1) the Bible records God's judgment against the sin of homosexuality from its first mention in Scripture; (2) people who are homosexual are somehow inferior in moral character and incapable of rising to the level of full heterosexual "Christian civilization"; and (3) people who are homosexual are willfully sinful, often sexually promiscuous and threatening, and deserve punishment for their own acts.

The church is once again repeating the mistakes of the past. And, as I will show in subsequent chapters, the reason why many people fail to apply Jesus' gospel to the issue of homosexuality is that they are once again using a "common sense" method of biblical interpretation and are following the lead of fundamentalist theologians whose methods are similar to those of Turretin.

We are thankful that most Christians no longer believe in racial and gender hierarchy. Why? What changed our minds? How was the church able to change? In the next chapter we will review the way in which a new, Christ-centered approach to biblical interpretation carried forth the best insights of the dissenting abolitionists and expanded and applied them. This christological approach, which used the whole Bible, with Jesus as its central character and interpreter, enabled the church to change its mind and heart on issues of race and women. Let us examine this new approach.

3

A Breakthrough in Understanding
the Word of God

HOW THE CHURCH CHANGED ITS MIND

How was the church able to change its mind on racial segregation and women's rights? White men in the mainstream churches had great power to claim that their experience was normative for all. After all, they held all the positions of power in church and in state. They interpreted reality according to their experience of being in a privileged position in society. That gave them the freedom to label others as inferior. Through their complete domination of society, they were able to pass off their biases as "common sense."

By the middle of the nineteenth century, the mainstream U.S. Protestant consensus on interpretation of the Bible fragmented.[1] Two events were crucial. One was the Civil War, in which Christians were divided north and south on biblical interpretation regarding slavery. The other was the publication of Darwin's *Origin of the Species* in 1859. Responses to Darwin's theory of evolution tended to separate people within the mainstream Protestant churches into two camps.

Those who came to be called modernists felt obliged to embrace the new science. They believed that the human race was moving toward God, Scripture represented the evolving experience of humankind, and creeds were only a human attempt to express religious experience.

Others, who came to be called fundamentalists, in contrast, believed that God had created the world once and for all in a certain way, the

Bible contained God's literal words as recorded by humans, and creeds represented a systematic presentation of doctrinal truths.[2]

Modernists and fundamentalists in these churches fought each other for decades over the meaning of Scripture. Modernists denied the authenticity of certain parts of the Bible, while fundamentalists insisted that the entire Bible, in the original manuscripts, was inerrant. By this, fundamentalists meant that God was the author of Scripture and therefore whatever the Bible said could be applied directly to present-day circumstances, overriding science if science conflicted with their own views of what was considered biblical. Modernists, in frustration, appealed to the scientific method of observation and experimentation as having greater authority for modern people.

The two dueling parties came to a stalemate in what was called the fundamentalist-modernist controversy of the early twentieth century. Fundamentalists in the Presbyterian Church had developed, and persuaded the denomination to adopt, a list of five "essential and necessary doctrines" that all candidates for ministry had to accept: (1) the inerrancy of Scripture, (2) Jesus' virgin birth, (3) his vicarious substitutionary atonement on the cross, (4) his bodily resurrection, and (5) the power of Jesus' mighty miracles.[3] Presbyterian General Assemblies in 1910, 1916, and 1923 made acceptance of the fundamentalists' five "essential and necessary doctrines" mandatory for all candidates for ordination to the ministry.

The decades-long fundamentalist-modernist conflict in the Presbyterian Church came to a crisis point at the General Assembly in 1925, when it appeared that the church might split. In response, the moderator, Charles Erdman, left the chair[4] and moved that a special commission be formed to discern the "causes of unrest" in the church. The leading spokespersons for the two competing parties both seconded the motion.

In 1927, this powerful commission proposed that no one, including the General Assembly, could create a short list of essential doctrines and demand adherence to them. The church's doctrine, the committee said, was to be found in its confessional statements, at that time the Westminster Confession of Faith and the Larger and Shorter Catechisms. If a person had a "scruple," or disagreement, it was up to the regional governing body, the presbytery, to adjudicate that conflict through the judicial process.[5]

The 1927 General Assembly overwhelmingly accepted the report of its commission. Affirmation of the five "essentials," including the inerrancy of the Bible, was no longer required for ordination.[6] However, the General Assembly never declared that the "essentials" were wrong and inconsistent with the Reformed tradition. Thus, an ambiguity resulted that has allowed some people ever since to appeal to these "fundamentals" as if they were authoritative and had only been bypassed by a decision on church government.

The opposite is actually true. The church at that time had a strong theological center. For example, in 1924, a large group of pastors signed a document called the Auburn Affirmation.[7] These influential church leaders included people of various persuasions regarding the "essentials." However, they all opposed the imposition of the five "essential and necessary doctrines" as church law. The signers of the Auburn Affirmation said they were able to distinguish between the "facts" of the Christian faith, to which they all adhered, and the "theories" embodied in the "essentials," about which they could disagree.[8]

Theology Guides Biblical Interpretation

Just as the fundamentalist-modernist controversy was concluding in the 1930s, a fresh theological breeze blew in from Europe. This theological movement broke the stalemate of the fundamentalist-modernist controversy and enabled the church to move forward in a renewed commitment to Christ.

The movement variously was called Neo-Calvinism, Neo-Protestantism, and Neo-Reformation theology.[9] The most familiar and most often used name was neo-orthodoxy. It was "neo" because it was a *new* approach that was not dependent on either fundamentalism or its modernist opponents. It was "orthodox" in that it turned people's attention to Jesus Christ as revealed in Scripture and depended on the work of the Holy Spirit to make the biblical message alive through preaching. Neo-orthodoxy focused on the traditional doctrines of the Christian faith, but looked at them afresh in the light of current scholarship.

The names of Swiss neo-orthodox theologians Karl Barth and Emil Brunner became common in American theological schools in the 1940s and 1950s.[10] These Neo-Reformation theologians encouraged people to study the sources of the Protestant movement, especially Calvin and Luther. Reading Reformation theologians, and the contemporary theologians who had been influenced by them, produced a new kind of theology that had reverence for the Bible and used all the tools of contemporary scholarship to understand it.

World War I, which had involved some of the most "civilized" countries in Europe, dashed the existing liberal optimism about human nature. Human effort, it appeared, was not bringing in God's kingdom, nor was human reason proving adequate to know God. Neo-orthodoxy's defining insight, taken from the Danish philosopher Søren Kierkegaard, was that people and God are known by personal encounter, not by rational analysis.[11] The revelation of God comes *not* in an inspired book, but in the person of Jesus Christ, who is God incarnate.[12] The Bible is a witness to Christ. Thus, this approach to biblical interpretation was called "christological." In illustration of this, a print of Mattheus Grünewald's Isenheim altarpiece from Colmar, France, hung over Barth's desk in Basel, Switzerland. In it, John the Baptist, symbolizing the role of the Bible, stands pointing a long, bony finger at Christ on the cross. Because the Bible, like John the Baptist, points away from itself to Christ, the issue of possible mistakes in the Bible was irrelevant to Barth. According to him, by the action of the Holy Spirit, through preaching, the Bible *becomes* the word of God to people of faith.

Neither modernism nor fundamentalism survived World War II intact. In World War II, modern science was again used to produce weapons that killed millions. Fascism in Europe demonstrated the danger of a rigid worldview that did not allow for diversity of opinions. People in Europe and America were ready for new ways to think about and experience God. Theologians in the mainstream churches welcomed the message of neo-orthodoxy. People were able to focus on Christ, to whom Scripture pointed, and at the same time were encouraged to use all the tools of scholarship to interpret the Bible.

Neo-orthodoxy offered a new approach to theology and biblical studies.[13] In biblical studies this shift in thinking was called the "biblical theology movement."[14] The difference between neo-orthodoxy and "biblical theology" was primarily in the academic disciplines practiced by their adherents. Neo-orthodoxy was the name applied to the views of systematic theologians and historians of doctrine. Scholars who studied the text of the Old Testament and/or the New Testament were part of the biblical theology movement.[15] The biblical scholars shared with the theologians both a concentration on the divine self-disclosure and a recognition of the very human element involved in recording historical events. Both stressed the uniqueness of biblical religion against the ancient Near Eastern background. They were open to all of the scientific biblical scholarship, while also insisting on one overarching theology proclaimed in the Bible.[16]

Biblical scholars influenced by neo-orthodoxy no longer debated reliable authority versus human authorship, as had been the case in the fundamentalist-modernist controversy. They did not view the Bible as a collection of inerrant facts, but as a very human document that reliably recorded a very real encounter of real people with a real God.[17] As biblical scholar Eugene March noted, "It seems clear in retrospect that the main concern among biblical theologians of the '40s and '50s was to declare the validity of biblical authority in such a way as to steer clear of the mistakes of both Liberalism and Fundamentalism."[18] Common Sense philosophy and the rationalism of Turretin, which had dominated theology in the preceding era, were now replaced by a more Christ-centered method of biblical interpretation.[19]

Some fundamentalists reacted strongly against the rise of a new theological perspective. In 1940, a Charlotte, North Carolina, businessman named Tom Glasgow attacked E. T. Thompson, a professor at Union Theological Seminary, for failing to maintain what Glasgow considered the traditional interpretation of the faith. Glasgow believed that the theology of Charles Hodge and B. B. Warfield, professors at Princeton in the nineteenth and early twentieth centuries, should remain normative for the church. Regarding the inspiration of the Bible, Glasgow agreed with the Old Princeton position that the Bible was "an oracular Book, as the Word of God, in such a sense that whatever it says, God says."[20]

Since Glasgow refused to press formal charges of heresy in the church courts, Thompson was given no opportunity to defend himself; so Thompson asked his presbytery to examine him. The presbytery did so and found Thompson not guilty of the charges alleged against him. This judgment was precedent-setting in that it specifically denied that a theological professor had to accept the interpretation of the confessions made by his predecessors.[21] This decision marked the beginning of a gradual sea change in the southern Presbyterian Church in its attitude toward both biblical inerrancy and the Old Princeton interpretation of the Westminster Confession.

SOCIAL CHANGE

The influence of neo-orthodoxy and the biblical theology movement enabled the church to take a fresh look at oppressive social institutions. Theologians, and the pastors whom they had taught, no longer were bound by Turretin's theology or Scottish Common Sense philosophy. Instead of proof-texting, that is, taking particular verses out of their context and treating them as universal laws, they looked at the totality of the Bible in its cultural context. They began with Jesus Christ. Each passage of the Bible was viewed through the lens of Jesus' redemptive life and ministry. From that starting point, and stimulated by changes in American society, church leaders began to rethink controversial social issues.

A New Look at Race

Social and cultural events soon provided an occasion for the new biblical understandings of social issues to be put into practice. When, on May 17, 1954, the United States Supreme Court, in *Brown v. Board of Education,* ordered desegregation of the public schools, the southern Presbyterian Church (PCUS) was ready. On May 27, its General Assembly affirmed the principle of the Supreme Court's decision and urged all members to support those charged with implementing it.[22] The assembly further adopted the recommendation of its Council of Christian Relations "that the General Assembly affirm that enforced segregation of the races is discrimination which is out of harmony with Christian theology and ethics." The assembly urged the church at all governing body levels, from the local session to the General Assembly, to be open to people of all races.[23]

The PCUS was the first major church body in the United States to embrace the Supreme Court decision. Many believed that the PCUS General Assembly was ready to condemn racial segregation even if the court had not spoken.[24]

Then, in 1956, a PCUS report on the biblical justification for the equality of women also clearly rejected the biblical justification of slavery. The committee, in its final statement on the principles of biblical interpretation, wrote:

> Coming closer to our own day, we no longer argue that human slavery is justified by the Bible, and in accord with God's will. Some of our grandfathers did so argue, declaring that slavery was God's permanent institution. Through the illumination of the Holy Spirit, we have come to a different understanding on this subject. We see that the Bible passages they quoted were not kept by them in the larger context of the Bible as a whole.[25]

This statement was a direct repudiation of Thornwell's 1861 theory that the particular text should have priority over the general principle. New methods of biblical interpretation focused on the Bible as a whole. The statement understood the Bible's central themes to be salvation and service, with the life and ministry of Christ as the central interpretive principle.

A New Look at the Role of Women

One of the best illustrations of the application of the new principles of biblical and confessional interpretation is found in the 1956 PCUS report on the status of women. Women had been ordained as elders since 1930 in the northern Presbyterian Church, and as ministers since 1956. In that year, their southern cousins were still struggling with ordination of women to office in the church. A committee dealing with the status of women developed an approach based on the denomination's confessional stance. They believed that a solution could be found in accord with the Westminster Confession of Faith's principle that "The infallible rule of interpretation of Scripture, is the Scripture itself; and therefore, when there is a question about the true and full sense of any scripture (which is not manifold, but one), it may be searched and known by other places that speak more clearly."[26]

The committee applied this principle by saying, "We find it clearly and unmistakably stated in Scripture that God endowed at least some women for leadership among His [sic] people in Bible days. Therefore, we conclude that what God has done, and has promised to do (Acts 2:17) may be done in our own day."[27]

Thus, Presbyterians in the 1950s reached back to the 1640s and drew from the Westminster Confession a principle that enabled them to apply the gospel to a new situation. Empowered with this more expansive understanding of God's will, southern Presbyterians made ordination to all offices of the church available to women and in 1965 ordained their first woman minister of Word and Sacrament.

A New Look at Divorce and Remarriage

The PCUSA and the PCUS reflected the ambivalence of both church members and ministers by, beginning in 1926, alternately (1) attempting to rigidify church law by prohibiting any divorce and then (2) expanding the exception clauses that allowed for divorce and remarriage. Over the next thirty years, the Presbyterian churches cautiously felt their way toward a new understanding of the meaning of marriage, which involved applying the new christological interpretation of Scripture that had taken hold after World War II.

Today's more pastoral attitude toward divorce and remarriage began when the Presbytery of Dubuque in 1929 reacted against the attempt of the previous General Assembly to eliminate all exceptions and forbid divorce in every instance. The Dubuque overture asserted that a strict legalism would "not solve the problem, but may cause hardship and injustice."[28]

In 1930 the PCUSA General Assembly received a thorough study of divorce and remarriage in the church. The Commission on Marriage, Divorce, and Remarriage took a spiritual, rather than legalistic, approach to both Scripture and the confessions. Jesus' attitude toward divorce, expressed in Matthew 19:3–13 and Mark 10:2–12, was presented as an ideal toward which young people should strive, for it embodied "the meaning and values of marriage."[29]

The commission's report did not ask for change in the existing standards, which recognized only two grounds for divorce—adultery or irremediable desertion—and allowed remarriage after divorce only for the innocent party in either case. It did, however, offer an expanded, spiritual understanding and application of the Westminster Confession and Catechisms: "Beyond the fact that the marriage relation is terminated by death, is the further fact that it may be destroyed by either party to the agreement proving unfaithful to the vows taken."[30] The commission concluded: "Anything that kills love and deals death to the spirit of the union is infidelity," citing the biblical phrase, "The letter killeth; but the spirit giveth life."[31] With this interpretation, the report introduced the concept of a moral equivalent of death to justify divorce.

Some twenty years later, after World War II, in 1952, the report of a Special Committee on Proposed Changes in the Confession of Faith stated that "remarriage after a divorce granted on grounds explicitly stated in Scripture or implicit in the gospel of Christ may be sanctioned in keeping with his redemptive gospel."[32] This provision called for revisions to the Westminster Confession of Faith, which were approved by the presbyteries and adopted by the PCUSA General Assembly in 1953. The changes allowed divorce and remarriage on these theological grounds.

During the same period the southern stream was engaged in a parallel struggle. In a 1929 attempt by a PCUS committee to eliminate "desertion" as a ground for divorce, the concept of moral equivalency was introduced. Dr. Charles E. Diehl, then president of Southwestern College in Memphis, argued, "We recognize the violation of the Seventh Commandment *or its moral equivalent* [emphasis added] as the only ground for divorce," and he suggested that desertion, "and perhaps some other causes, constitute what may be termed 'moral equivalent.'"[33]

In the aftermath of World War II, in 1945, the PCUS had received an overture asking the church to conduct a careful study of church laws on grounds for divorce and the procedure for remarriage.[34] In 1950, the Council of Christian Relations submitted its initial report on "Divorce and Remarriage." The report commented on biblical interpretation in a way that reflected the new PCUS approach, taken since World War II: "Any attempt to build a Christian doctrine of marriage and divorce on a few isolated 'proof-texts' will always fail for at least two reasons: (a) the usual proof-texts are open to more than one interpretation, and (b) they fail to give due weight to the implications of Jesus' total teaching with respect to man's [*sic*] personal responsibilities and social relationships."[35]

The report further noted that "infidelity can be spiritual as well as physical and it manifests itself in many forms. It is therefore unrealistic to hold that divorce is permissible only when marriage has been broken by one of two forms of infidelity, both of which are physical acts."[36] It concluded, "Wherever free Protestant churches are studying this problem today in the light of Jesus' total teachings on human relations, the trend is unmistakably away from a strictly legalistic approach to one more finely and fundamentally spiritual."[37]

The PCUS Council of Christian Relations reported to the 1952 assembly that limiting grounds for remarriage after divorce to adultery and desertion "may be doing grave injustice to a multitude of injured people who are victims of forces they could not control." In a spirit of honesty it observed that "in practice they [PCUS ministers] are ignoring the letter of our Church's law in order, as they see it, to be true to the spirit and total teachings of our Lord, to the practical realities of life and to the demands of Christian justice."[38]

In 1959, after fourteen years of debate within the church, the PCUS amended the Westminster Confession of Faith regarding divorce. The presbyteries overwhelmingly approved new wording that, although hedged with qualifiers and footnoted with numerous Scripture references,[39] was similar to the PCUSA revised section of the Westminster

Confession: "The remarriage of divorced persons may be sanctioned by the Church in keeping with the redemptive Gospel of Christ, when sufficient penitence for sin and failure is evident, and a firm purpose of and endeavor after Christian marriage is manifested."[40]

In the 1950s, both branches of American Presbyterianism took the remarkable step of revising the Westminster Confession of Faith on divorce and remarriage. In both cases, Presbyterians had shifted their emphasis from a public norm to the good of the people involved. The primary purpose of marriage was no longer the benefit of society but the benefit of the people entering the marriage covenant.[41]

The Presbyterian denominations had turned away from what they considered a legalistic approach to marriage and divorce based on a literal interpretation of biblical and confessional texts. Now they cited the spirit and totality of Jesus' teaching as mandating a pastoral approach that allowed exceptions to previous rules. This was solidified by changes made in the Confession of Faith.

How is this relevant to granting equality to gay and lesbian members of our churches? Jesus' words that divorce is equivalent to adultery are among the clearest statements on a moral issue in Scripture. The Westminster Confession was clear as well, although it did set a precedent for allowing exceptions in the case of adultery or desertion. If we were to take literally Jesus' teaching on divorce, we would still not be accepting divorced and remarried people as office bearers in the church. Yet church law now asks that we take literally less clear statements regarding homosexual behavior. It is a double standard: current church law permits a pastoral approach concerning marriage and divorce for people who are heterosexual and mandates a legalistic approach toward people who are homosexual.

We can learn from the way in which the Presbyterian churches, north and south, slowly shifted from legalistic proof-texting to looking at Scripture through the lens of Jesus' life and ministry. Jesus did not set forth immutable laws to break people. Rather, he set forth an ideal toward which we all should strive—lifelong faithfulness in married relationships. That ideal could apply to gay or lesbian couples as well as to heterosexual couples.[42]

A Personal Note

In 1952–53, I was a sophomore at the University of Nebraska. Debate was my principal extracurricular activity. That year the debate coaches suggested that I also try competition in oratory. As a young Christian I was very concerned with divorce and decided to work on that topic for my oration. As a member of the United Presbyterian Church of North America, I was unaware of the fierce debate concerning divorce and remarriage going on at that time in the PCUSA and PCUS denominations. To get experience that I could draw on, I attended divorce court on the day before Christmas, 1952. I expected to see some fiery emotional outbursts. Instead I was struck with how quickly and easily divorce could take place. As I said in the oration, "I was startled to realize that a partnership which was supposed to last for life, had been terminated while a choir was singing three verses of a Christmas hymn."[43]

I took a very hard line on divorce in that oration. I asserted, "To protect people against themselves, we must make the laws so strict that divorce is almost impossible. . . . For those couples who no longer wished to live together, but whose circumstances were not exceptional, there would be legal separation."[44]

I see things differently now. The northern and southern Presbyterian denominations learned something in the 1950s. I have learned the same lessons since. Jesus' statements in Matthew 19 and Mark 10 are not an inflexible law intended to separate sinners from the righteous. Instead, Jesus is showing us an ideal that offers hope to all of us. I count many divorced people and remarried Christian couples as my friends. I thank God for who they are and for the wholeness they have experienced. It is helpful and humbling to realize that I can change my mind on something about which I was once so sure.

Consolidating the Theological Consensus in a Confession

The theological consensus of neo-orthodoxy and the biblical theology movement in the 1940s, 1950s, and 1960s enabled the Presbyterian denominations for the first time in 200 years to reject discrimination against African Americans and women and to deal more personally and pastorally with divorced and remarried people. The churches then moved to consolidate that consensus on biblical interpretation by embodying it in a confession of faith.

The process, for Presbyterians in the North, began in 1956 when the Presbytery of Amarillo (PCUSA) overtured the General Assembly asking that the Westminster Shorter Catechism be rewritten in contemporary language. An assembly-appointed committee, after a year of reflection, proposed an alternative: That a committee be named to draft "a brief contemporary statement of faith to be included in the Constitution after the union is consummated in 1958." (This 1958 union was of the Presbyterian Church, U.S.A. [PCUSA] and the United Presbyterian Church of North America [UPCNA]. The resulting church was named the United Presbyterian Church in the United States of America [UPCUSA].)

The rationale for this new statement of faith was that "It should bring to all members of our Church some sense of participation in the thrilling revival of theology." That "thrilling revival" was, of course, the neo-orthodox and biblical theology movement consensus that had begun to develop in the 1940s and 1950s.[45]

In 1958 the uniting General Assembly named nine men to a Committee on a Brief Contemporary Statement of Faith. Edward A. Dowey Jr. of Princeton Theological Seminary was appointed the chair. Over the next four years, eleven members, including one woman, ruling elder Mrs. E. Harris Harbison, were added to the committee as some of the original members dropped out.[46] Most of the members of the committee had been shaped by the return to Reformation roots fostered by the neo-orthodox revival of the '40s and '50s.

For chairman Dowey and most of the committee, as for Barth, what mattered was revelation in the person, Jesus Christ. Neo-orthodoxy, they believed, would rescue the Scriptures from the Old Princeton doctrine of the inerrancy of the Bible.

In 1966 a revision committee was appointed at the General Assembly, which had the power to amend the new confession of faith submitted in 1965. A compromise was reached between those on the original drafting committee, who wanted to speak only of Jesus Christ as the Word of God, and those on the revision committee, who insisted on also speaking of Scripture as the Word of God. The final draft on Scripture in the resulting Confession of 1967 reads, "The one sufficient revelation of God is Jesus Christ, the Word of God incarnate, to whom the Holy Spirit bears unique and authoritative witness through the Holy Scriptures, which are received and obeyed as the word of God written." A capital *W* was used when Christ was referred to as the Word of God, a lowercase *w* for word of God in reference to Scripture.[47] The compromise held, and the Confession was adopted.

The Social Effects of the Confession of 1967

In the Confession of 1967 a christological interpretation of Scripture was the basis of a commitment to racial reconciliation. The authors of the Confession of 1967 believed that God's reconciling work in Jesus Christ was the heart of the gospel in any age and that the church of that generation was especially called to the ministry of reconciliation.[48] Referring to racial discrimination, the Confession of 1967 said, "God has created the people of the earth to be one universal family. In his reconciling love, he overcomes the barriers between brothers [*sic*] and breaks down every form of discrimination based on racial or ethnic difference, real or imaginary. . . . Therefore, the church labors for the abolition of all racial discrimination and ministers to those injured by it."[49]

This new christological hermeneutic also took root in the South. In 1976 the PCUS General Assembly adopted "A Declaration of Faith" that said, "When we encounter apparent tensions and conflicts in what Scripture teaches us to believe and do, the final appeal must be to the authority of Christ."[50] On race, the declaration said, "The antagonisms between races, nations and neighbors, . . . are manifestations of our sin against God."[51] A christological interpretation of Scripture finally overcame the Presbyterian Church's silence on the sin of slavery and racial segregation.

Theological Backlash: Women's Ordination

By 1965, women in the Presbyterian Church, both north and south, had been admitted to all of the offices of the church—deacon, elder, and minister of Word and Sacrament. Yet pockets of resistance to women's leadership remained. When the United Presbyterian Church of North America united with the Presbyterian Church in the U.S.A. in 1958, one very large issue was never publicly discussed and was left unresolved: The UPCNA did not ordain women as either elders or ministers.

This unresolved issue erupted in the 1970s in a celebrated case involving Walter Wynn Kenyon, a senior at Pittsburgh Seminary. Kenyon was one of a group of students who were staunch followers of Professor John H. Gerstner Jr., who taught a form of Calvinism that was an extension of the Old Princeton theology of Charles Hodge and B. B. Warfield. One of the convictions of this group was that the Bible "clearly teaches women should be subordinate ('silent') in the official teaching and ruling ministry of the Christian Church."[52]

Gerstner's followers, including Kenyon, contended that the matter of women's ordination was a nonessential detail of the Presbyterian system of doctrine and governance. Therefore they felt free, in the language of the Adopting Act of 1729, to "scruple" against, or disagree with, this point and yet be ministers in good standing in the denomination.[53] In that spirit, Kenyon made clear to the Candidates and Credentials Committee of Pittsburgh Presbytery that he believed that the Bible forbade the ordination of women.

The Candidates and Credentials Committee recommended against ordaining Kenyon because he could not affirmatively answer question five (of the eight) ordination questions: "Do you endorse our Church's government, and will you honor its discipline? Will you be a friend among your comrades in ministry, working with them, subject to the ordering of God's word and Spirit?"[54]

Kenyon, Gerstner, and several colleagues wrote a pamphlet explaining and defending their position:

> Our purpose is simply to demonstrate what we believe to be the real issue: Biblical authority. . . . The Scriptures consistently teach that in the church and in the home women are placed in a subordinate position. No one can read the Bible and not see authority 'writ large' therein. Everywhere we meet a chain of command. . . . Everyone who loves and fears God should acknowledge that the Word of God authoritatively establishes authority—male authority—in the church.[55]

The presbytery overruled its committee and recommended ordination for Kenyon. That decision was appealed to the synod, which then reversed the presbytery and recommended that Kenyon not be ordained. In turn, the synod's ruling was appealed to the Permanent Judicial Commission (PJC) of the General Assembly, which upheld the synod's decision not to ordain Kenyon.

In its 1974 decision, the Permanent Judicial Commission in the Kenyon Case cited the Confession of 1967. The PJC decision stated that the equality of women and men is an essential of Presbyterian theological beliefs: "The question of the importance of our belief in the equality of all people before God is thus essential to the disposition of this case. It is evident from our Church's confessional standards that the Church believes the Spirit of God has led us into new understandings of this equality before God."[56]

This decision, affirming the equality of women and men in church leadership, was based on the insight of the Confession of 1967 concerning the equality of people of all races. The PJC quoted the Confession of 1967: "Congregations, individuals, or groups of Christians who exclude, dominate, or patronize their fellowmen [sic], however subtly, resist the Spirit of God and bring contempt on the faith which they profess."[57] The PJC followed that citation by declaring, "The UPCUSA, in obedience to Jesus Christ, under the authority of Scripture (and guided by its confessions) has now developed its understanding of the equality of all people (both male and female) before God."[58] Here we see the method of biblical interpretation that took hold in the 1940s and was embodied in the Confession of 1967 enabling the church to reject the older literalist method of interpreting Scripture.

A Brief Statement of Faith on Women

In 1991 the equality of women and men was given explicit confessional status. The Articles of Agreement that governed the 1983 reunion of the PCUS with the UPCUSA mandated that the reuniting assembly instruct its moderator to appoint a committee "representing diversities of points of view and groups within the reunited Church to prepare a Brief Statement of the Reformed Faith for possible inclusion in *The Book of Confessions*."[59]

This committee was unique in the history of Reformed creedal formation in two ways. First, the group was chosen specifically for its diversity and then expected to write a document evoking unity. Second, it was the first time that a significant number of women were members of a committee engaged in preparing a Reformed confessional document.

Most importantly, for the first time in Reformed creedal history, women were declared equal to men and were affirmed to be called to all of the ministries of the church. In the PC(USA) *Book of Confessions*, A Brief Statement of Faith made explicit the equality of all people: "In sovereign love God created the world good and makes everyone equally in God's image, male and female, of every race and people, to live as one community."[60] A Brief Statement of Faith also provided clear confessional warrant for the ordination of women, declaring that the Spirit "calls women and men to all the ministries of the Church."[61]

For some, the confession's most startling innovation was its use of feminine as well as masculine language to refer to God: "Loving us still, God makes us heirs with Christ of the covenant. Like a mother who will not forsake her nursing child, like a father who runs to welcome the prodigal home, God is faithful still."[62] The statements comparing God to a mother and a father are taken directly from the biblical text; mother is from Isaiah 49:15–16, father from Luke 15:11–32.

This use of metaphorical language also sharply contrasts with a naive literalism in the use of biblical language. The writers of A Brief Statement of Faith knew that God is neither male nor female. They acknowledged that we use human illustrations to point beyond ourselves to the reality of a personal God whose love exceeds that of our best human examples.[63]

LEARNING FROM OUR THEOLOGICAL, SOCIAL, AND CONFESSIONAL PAST

Guided by neo-orthodoxy in the 1940s and '50s, the church began to deal responsibly with social issues. Under the influence of a Christ-centered understanding of Scripture, the church spoke out against racial segregation, ordained women, and allowed divorced and remarried people to have full rights of church membership.

Now, however, faced with the issue of homosexuality, many churches are repeating the mistakes of the past. When churches meet a new situation where oppressed people are questioning the cultural status quo, many people instinctively become defensive and retreat. To justify their inability to cope with cultural change, they turn to the Bible and proof-text, that is they take verses out of the context of the whole and make universal laws of them. Instead of reading the Bible through the lens of Jesus' life and ministry, many have again tried to make the Bible a law book, which they then apply selectively, only to those with whom they disagree.

This need not be the case. When Christians read the Bible through the lens of Jesus' gracious life and ministry, they will be able to see lesbian, gay, bisexual, and transgender people as their sisters and brothers, faced with all the usual human problems, and loved equally by God.

The method of biblical interpretation that neo-orthodoxy introduced in the 1940s was rooted in the methods of biblical interpretation used by the sixteenth-century Protestant Reformers. When Barth, Brunner, and others encouraged American Presbyterians to read Calvin and Luther, scholars began to discover a heritage that had been obscured by the nineteenth-century Princeton theology. Reid's Common Sense philosophy and Turretin's theological system both came after the sixteenth-century Reformers and the development of the Westminster Confession of Faith. So, what was new in the 1940s led theologians and biblical scholars back to an earlier Reformation heritage.

In the early 1980s Presbyterians reaffirmed that heritage and used the principles of biblical interpretation found in the Reformed confessions to formulate principles, or guidelines, of biblical interpretation for use in theological controversies. These guidelines, if followed, will be extremely useful in dealing with the controversy over whether homosexual members of the church are permitted the full rights of membership.

In the next chapter we will examine these guidelines, their confessional origins, and their application to people who are homosexual. Upholding our best principles and practices in interpreting the Bible will help us to move forward together as a community of faith.

4

Interpreting the Bible in Times of Controversy

Presbyterians have a very orthodox official position on the authority and interpretation of the Bible![1]

In 1982 and 1983 both the northern and southern Presbyterian churches adopted guidelines for the interpretation of Scripture. The reports of the two denominations were self-consciously harmonious because, at root, they were both based on study of the Reformed confessions. They were published together by the reunited PC(USA) in 1992 with the comment, "The two papers were written in response to the need for a common basis in a diverse church for understanding and using Scripture."[2]

These principles of biblical interpretation are not exclusive to Presbyterians. They are essentially the same principles that are used by most mainstream Christian denominations today. They come from our common heritage in the Protestant Reformation.

Moving beyond Neo-orthodoxy

By the time the Confession of 1967 was adopted by the United Presbyterian Church, the era of neo-orthodoxy was nearing an end. By 1970 it was clear that there were new and important issues that Karl Barth and the other neo-orthodox scholars had not addressed: cultural pluralism; feminism; the rising consciousness of the two-thirds world; the reassertion of science, especially the social sciences.

Neo-orthodoxy had opened a new understanding of Scripture that was both Christ-centered and open to scholarly study of the texts. However, the distinctive element of neo-orthodoxy, which said that only Christ was the Word of God and that Scripture was only a witness to Christ, no longer seemed helpful.

Following the Reformed confessions, the guidelines adopted in the 1980s affirmed that while Jesus Christ is the living Word, the Bible was appropriately called the written Word of God.[3] Scholarly attention turned to giving the most careful and prayerful attention to the written Word in order to discover God's saving message in Christ.

By paying the closest attention to these human words in their historical and cultural context, the UPCUSA report in 1982 noted, we are helped to understand the divine message that speaks to our human condition, rather than only to a particular historical situation in the ancient Near East.[4] That report concluded, "Openness to the Holy Spirit's leading, as well as the tools of scholarship, implemented in faith and love, must be operative to yield the application of the message, especially in areas of controversy."[5]

Ironically, while the guidelines were intended to be used in times of controversy, by the time the denominational reports were finally published in 1992, in the debate over homosexuality people were already entrenched in positions that looked all too much like those of the bad, old fundamentalist-modernist conflict. Indeed, some people still seemed to want to replay that unhelpful fight.

Using these guidelines will not guarantee that we will all immediately agree. However, we can at least be sure that we are talking about the same thing and that we are looking at all we can learn from the Bible, not just one narrow slice of it. With that common understanding, we may find a common way forward. That is my prayer.

SEVEN GUIDELINES FOR INTERPRETATION

In the discussion that follows I first present each guideline. Then I cite its origins in the Reformed confessions. Finally, I discuss the interpretive principles involved and how each guideline might help us in our current debate concerning homosexuality. I use the 1982 UPCUSA guidelines, because they are a bit simpler and I am more familiar with them. I also incorporate insights from the 1983 PCUS document and its helpful confessional citations.

Let us go to these recommended guidelines for "a positive and not a restrictive use of Scripture in matters of controversy."[6]

> **Guideline #1. "Recognize that Jesus Christ, the Redeemer, is the center of Scripture. The redemptive activity of God is central to the entire Scripture. The Old Testament themes of the covenant and the messiah testify to this activity. In the center of the New Testament is Jesus Christ: the Word made flesh, the fulfillment of Israel's messianic hope, and the promise of the Kingdom. It is to Christ that the church witnesses. When interpreting Scripture, keeping Christ in the center aids in evaluating the significance of the problems and controversies that always persist in the vigorous, historical life of the church."[7]**

Confessional Origin

As the following statements show, our Reformed heritage affirms that Christ is the central interpretative principle of Scripture:

Calvin, in his commentary on John 12:48: *"In our reading of Scripture we shall hold simply to that which speaks clearly and definitely to our conscience and makes us feel that it leads us to Christ."*[8]

The Geneva Confession of 1541, concerning how we have the *"right knowledge of God,"* the knowledge that tells us God loves us and desires to be our Father and Savior: *"By his Word, in which he declares his mercy to us in Christ, and assures us of His love toward us."*[9]

The Synod of Berne (1528): *"But where something is brought before us by our pastors or by others which brings us closer to Christ . . . we will gladly accept it and will not limit the course of the Holy Spirit."*[10]

The Scots Confession (1560): *"When controversy arises about the right understanding of any passage or sentence of Scripture, or for the reformation of any abuse within the Kirk of God, we ought not so much to ask what men have said or done before us, as what the Holy Ghost uniformly speaks within the body of the Scriptures and what Christ Jesus himself did and commanded."*[11]

The Theological Declaration of Barmen, written in Germany against Nazi interference in the church (1934): *"Jesus Christ, as he is attested for us in Holy Scripture, is the one Word of God which we have to hear and which we have to trust and obey in life and in death.*"[12]

The Confession of 1967: *"The Bible is to be interpreted in light of its witness to God's work of reconciliation in Christ."*[13]

A Declaration of Faith, adopted by the General Assembly of the PCUS in 1976, but not approved by the three-fourths of the presbyteries required for it to be included in the *Book of Confessions*; nonetheless it is widely used in the denomination: *"Jesus Christ stands at the center of the biblical record."*[14]

Commentary

The Bible is about God and what God is doing in the world. Jesus is central to that story. For Christians, Jesus is the Christ, the Messiah, the incarnation of God in our world.

This message is at the heart of what the church believes and what I believe. Some years ago, I was preaching on the classical text about biblical inspiration in 2 Timothy 3:16, 17: "All scripture is inspired by God and is useful . . . so that everyone who belongs to God may be proficient, equipped for every good work." As I was preaching, I became increasingly aware of three boys, about ten years old, sitting in a front pew on my right, with no parental supervision. They weren't being bad, but they were pretty wiggly. So, suddenly I stopped and addressed the boys: "Boys, I can tell you everything the Bible is about in the next ten seconds. Why don't you time me?" This is what I said: "God made a good world. We messed it and ourselves up. God came in Jesus to put us and it back together again." One of those ten-year-old boys stood right up in church and said, "Nine seconds!" At least I had his attention for nine seconds.

The Bible is a story, and its central character is Jesus Christ. Thus the Bible is in some ways like a novel or a play. Its plot is creation, fall, and redemption—the outline of the Christian story.

Approaching the Bible through the lens of Jesus' life and ministry is not an easy task. It would be much simpler to live according to the black-and-white Hebrew laws of the Old Testament. But Jesus was not a legalist. In order to follow Jesus, we are called upon to show love for God, our neighbors, and even our enemies. Jesus showed love even for the outcasts of society. It is demanding and humbling to try to follow his example.

Can you imagine Jesus turning away someone who is despised, discriminated against, and distraught to the point of attempting suicide? I cannot. Yet some in the church have done just that to Christians who are homosexual.[15] When we keep our focus on Jesus, we will be able to come to a deeper understanding of the gospel. Then we need to pray for grace to see everyone in this discussion of homosexuality as our sister and brother in Christ.

Guideline #2. "Let the focus be on the plain text of Scripture, to the grammatical and historical context, rather than to allegory or subjective fantasy."

Confessional Origin

John Calvin: *"There are many statements in Scripture the meaning of which depends upon their context."*[16]

The Second Helvetic Confession (1566): *"But we hold that interpretation of the Scripture to be orthodox and genuine which is gleaned . . . (from the nature of the language in which they were written, likewise according to the circumstances in which they were set down)."*[17]

The Confession of 1967: *"The Scriptures, given under the guidance of the Holy Spirit, are nevertheless the words of men, conditioned by the language, thought forms, and literary fashions of the places and times at which they were written. They reflect views of life, history, and the cosmos which were then current. The church, therefore, has an obligation to approach the Scriptures with literary and historical understanding."*[18]

A Declaration of Faith (1976): *"God has chosen to address his inspired Word to us through diverse and varied human writings. Therefore we use the best available methods to understand them in their historical and cultural settings and the literary forms in which they are cast."*[19]

Commentary

This guideline warns against reading into Scripture what we want it to say. In medieval times, allegorism was a popular method that allowed one to find as many as seven levels of meaning in a text behind its plain meaning. Just as we must avoid a surface literalism, so we must avoid this sort of subjectivism that brings our biases to the text. We must, instead, take seriously the text as it is given to us and seek to understand it fully in its context.

The 1983 PCUS study indicates that to do justice to the plain text we must

1. define the appropriate literary units (passages, paragraphs, pericopes, etc.),
2. recognize the cultural conditioning of the language, and
3. understand the social and historical circumstances of the writing.

That means, for example, "Epic poetry is not historical chronicle; symbolic stories are not science; and admonition to a particular person or community is not general law."[20] Our Reformed confessions confirm these principles.

The "plain text" is "plain" only in its context. That means that it always requires responsible interpretation. Regarding homosexuality, we do well to heed the warning given in the PCUS "Guidelines": "While a particular text may name a subject with which we are also concerned in the present, the assumption should not be immediately made that the contemporary subject is the same as that addressed in the biblical text or that the circumstances and conditions of the biblical writer and modern interpreter are similar."[21]

For example, it seems wise to ask whether biblical statements that condemn idolatrous and immoral sexual activity can appropriately be applied to the sexual relationships of contemporary Christian gay and lesbian people who are neither idolatrous nor immoral. Is it right to take verses that condemn the worship of other gods and use them against Christian people who are worshipping the one true God whom Jesus called us to worship?

New Testament scholar Richard Hays notes that there is not "an exact equivalent for 'homosexual' in either Greek or Hebrew."[22] The Bible, in its original Hebrew and Greek, has no concept like our present understanding of a person with a homosexual orientation. Indeed, the concept of an ongoing sexual attraction to people of one's own sex did not exist in European or American language until the late nineteenth century.[23]

To be faithful to the "plain text" of Scripture, we must be very careful to understand the meaning of the text in its original context. Then we must be equally careful to discern if it is appropriate to apply that text in a quite different, contemporary context.

Guideline #3. "Depend on the guidance of the Holy Spirit in interpreting and applying God's message."

Confessional Origin

The Westminster Confession: *"We acknowledge the inward illumination of the Spirit of God to be necessary for the saving understanding of such things as are revealed in the Word."*[24]

The Westminster Confession: *"The Supreme Judge, by which all controversies of religion are to be determined, and all decrees of councils, opinions of ancient writers, doctrines of men, and private spirits, are to be examined, and in whose sentence we are to rest, can be no other but the Holy Spirit speaking in the Scripture."*[25]

The Confession of 1967: *"God's word is spoken to his church today where the Scriptures are faithfully preached and attentively read in dependence on the illumination of the Holy Spirit and with readiness to receive their truth and direction."*[26]

Commentary

Calvin promised that the "inner testimony of the Holy Spirit," which persuades us of the authority of Scripture, also assists us in interpreting Scripture. How? Not by giving us new information, but rather by giving a receptive attitude. With this attitude we can see, in the plain text, the essential message that God wants us to receive.

The Holy Spirit sometimes provides us with a new understanding of Scripture. The PCUS approach to biblical interpretation insists that "the confessions understand well that the church's traditional interpretation of Scripture is fallible and subject always to revision and correction."[27] The Holy Spirit has continually inspired change in the Christian church. The Spirit leads us into new beliefs and behaviors. This ability to change has enabled the church to cope with the changing world and to reach out to new people with the message of God's love in Christ. The early disciples in Jerusalem heard and accepted the reports of Peter and Paul that the Holy Spirit had descended on Gentiles (Acts 10 and 15), an idea that was previously unthinkable. Much of the Judaism in which they had been raised was based on the need to be separate from Gentiles, but the apostles and elders in Jerusalem changed their minds, and the church expanded.[28]

Christians in early America read their Bibles as saying that they should obey kings. But by the time of the American Revolution, people no longer took that admonition literally. Similarly, Christian people for centuries assumed that their Bibles condoned slavery and the subordination of women to men. Yet, over time and often reluctantly, people came to follow the Holy Spirit's leading to accept people of African origin and women as full and equal members of the church.

It seems that the Holy Spirit is once again working to change our church—making us restless, challenging us to give up our culturally conditioned prejudices against people of homosexual orientation. As we come to know faithful, obedient Christian disciples whose sexual orientation is different from that of the heterosexual majority, we discover that they have been blessed by the Holy Spirit even as heterosexual people have been. Under the guidance of the Holy Spirit, a change in our attitudes and actions can be a faithful response to God's leading.

Guideline #4. "Be guided by the doctrinal consensus of the church, which is the rule of faith."

Confessional Origin

The Heidelberg Catechism, Question and Answer 22: Q. *"What, then, must a Christian believe? A. All that is promised us in the gospel, a summary of which is taught us in the articles of the Apostles' Creed, our universally acknowledged confession of faith."*[29]

Most of the Reformation-era confessions, and even Calvin's *Institutes*, are elaborations on the Apostles' Creed, the Ten Commandments, and the Lord's Prayer, as is the Presbyterian adult Study Catechism approved in 1998 by the General Assembly for use in congregations.

The Second Helvetic Confession, confirming the importance of referring to the doctrinal consensus of the church: *"The apostle Peter has said that the Holy Scriptures are not of private interpretation (II Pet. 1:20), and thus we do not allow all possible interpretations."*[30]

The 1983 PCUS report, "Presbyterian Understanding and Use of Holy Scripture," stating that the Scriptures are always to be interpreted by and in the community of the church, the body of Christ: *"Since the guidance of the Holy Spirit is promised to individual Christians for the sake of building up and equipping the community of Christians for its mission in the world, the church's consensus is likely to be more accurate than the opinions of individual persons."*[31]

Commentary

The "rule of faith" refers to the doctrinal consensus of the church developed over time. When you read the affirmations of faith in the creeds, confessions, and catechisms of the church, such as those in the Presbyterian *Book of Confessions*, you cannot help but notice the amazing continuity of the essentials of the Christian message. There naturally are differences among the documents because of the different historical and cultural contexts in which they were developed, yet they all basically tell the same story. That is because each of them is reflecting a faithful response to the same biblical story. Thus we are given a solid footing on which to stand as we adapt the "old, old story" to new and changing circumstances.

At first glance, it might appear that the consensus of the church has been against the full acceptance of people who are homosexual. We must remember, however, that until very recently it was the practice of the Western church to deny full rights of membership to people of color and to women. Past practice is not necessarily a recommendation for future faithfulness. We must continue to distinguish between the culturally conditioned practices of the church and the essential teachings of the church found in its creedal statements, which are the "rule of faith."

The Reformed confessions, properly translated, say nothing about homosexuality.[32] In fact, they say very little about sexuality itself. The Nicene and the Apostles' creeds make no mention of sexuality. A Brief Statement of Faith, 1991, makes no mention, and the same is true of the Scots Confession. The Barmen Declaration of 1934 makes no mention of sexual relations. The Heidelberg Catechism says that we should *"live chaste and disciplined lives, whether in holy wedlock or in single life."*[33] The Second Helvetic Confession speaks of those *"who have the gift of celibacy from heaven,"* but notes that *"if the gift be taken away,"* they should feel free to marry. It speaks at length about marriage and condemns polygamy. At the same time, it rebukes those who condemn second marriages.[34] The Westminster Confession outlaws divorce, but it allows exceptions for the *"innocent party"* in cases of adultery or desertion. The Westminster Larger Catechism, in chronicling the sins forbidden in the prohibition of adultery, broadens the list to include *"all unclean imaginations, thoughts, purposes, and affections."*[35] In listing the duties required by the Seventh Commandment, it includes *"conjugal love and cohabitation."*[36]

The original draft of the Confession of 1967 focused on three global problems: racial discrimination; enslaving poverty in a world of abundance; and the need for peace, justice, and freedom among nations.[37] The revision committee added a fourth issue: anarchy in sexual relationships,[38] citing human beings' *"perennial confusion about the meaning of sex"* and stressing that this confusion *"has been aggravated in our day."* It then notes seemingly opposite pressures such as *"new means of birth control,"* and *"world overpopulation."*[39]

Our creedal "rule of faith" makes clear that opinions about homosexuality are not essential matters of faith.

> **Guideline #5. "Let all interpretations be in accord with the rule of love, the two-fold commandment to love God and to love our neighbor."**

Confessional Origin

The Scots Confession: *"We dare not receive or admit any interpretation which is contrary to any principal point of our faith, or to any other plain text of Scripture, or to the rule of love."*[40]

The Second Helvetic Confession: *"We hold that interpretation of the Scripture to be orthodox and genuine which . . . agree[s] with the rule of faith and love, and contributes much to the glory of God and man's salvation."*[41]

Commentary

When we interpret Scripture in a way that is hurtful to people, we can be sure that we are not glorifying God. "You will know them by their fruits" was Jesus' criterion for judging false prophets (Matt. 7:16). Whether our interpretations of Scripture result in love for God and neighbor is a practical test of whether our interpretation is correct.

Treating everyone by the same just and loving standard would seem to be a criterion for the application of our interpretations of Scripture. The PCUS report in 1983 notes, "No interpretation of Scripture is correct that leads to or supports contempt for any individual or group of persons either within or outside of the church." Further, it states, "Any interpretation of Scripture is wrong that separates or sets in opposition love for God and love for fellow human being."[42]

Walter Wink, professor of New Testament at Auburn Seminary, states:

The crux of the matter, it seems to me, is simply that the Bible has no sexual ethic. Instead, it exhibits a variety of sexual mores, some of which changed over the thousand-year span of biblical history. Mores are unreflective customs accepted by a given community. Many of the practices that the Bible prohibits, we allow, and many that it allows, we prohibit. The Bible knows only a love ethic, which is constantly being brought to bear on whatever sexual mores are dominant in any given country, or culture, or period.[43]

> **Guideline #6.** "Remember that interpretation of the Bible requires earnest study in order to establish the best text and to interpret the influence of the historical and cultural context in which the divine message has come."

Confessional Origin

The Westminster Confession of Faith, in chapter 1 on Scripture, subsection 7, on what we know by experience: *"All things in Scripture are not alike plain in themselves, nor alike clear unto all; yet those things which are necessary to be known, believed, and observed, for salvation, are so clearly propounded and opened in some place of Scripture or other, that not only the learned, but the unlearned, in a due use of the ordinary means, may attain unto a sufficient understanding of them."*[44]

The most important notion above is that only beliefs having to do with salvation are both essential and clear.

Subsection 8 announces that in "controversies of religion" we are to study Greek and Hebrew and, by extension, the historical and cultural context of the passages in question.[45]

In saying that we require earnest study, especially regarding controversies of religion, we imply that our ideas and/or our behavior could be wrong. The Westminster Confession: *"All synods and councils since the apostles' times, whether general or particular, may err, and many have erred; therefore they are not to be made the rule of faith or practice, but to be used as a help in both."*[46]

The Scots Confession, preface: *"We protest that if any man will note in this confession of ours any article or sentence repugnant to God's holy word, that it would please him of his gentleness and for Christian charity's sake to admonish us of the same in writing.*"[47]

Commentary

Establishing the "best text" means doing the arduous work of comparing ancient manuscripts of the biblical material in order to establish a Bible that is as close to the original as possible. At the time of the Protestant Reformation much scholarly work remained to be done to compile a basic text on which all scholars could agree. Today scholars have compared such a large number of manuscripts that they feel fairly certain that they are very close to what the original text must have been, and thus are working with a generally authentic biblical text.[48]

When we move to the question of interpretation, again we have a strong consensus on the central message of the Bible. Scripture has a clear central saving message of creation, fall, and redemption in Christ. Sometimes Christians have had difficulty differentiating the surrounding cultural milieu from that central saving message. Describing these two different aspects of biblical literature is a task for biblical scholarship. We need to use the ministry of those who are experts in ancient languages, cultures, and philosophies to understand nuances of ancient Middle Eastern thought and practice that we encounter in the Bible.

God's message did not come to us in a fax from heaven. God dealt with real people who lived in particular cultures, and those cultures shaped the ways in which people understood and applied their understandings of God's word to them. Practices that we now rightly reject, including polygamy and slavery, were taken for granted in ancient cultures. Scholarly study can help us discern the difference between, on the one hand, something that is there in Scripture just because it was an accepted part of the culture and, on the other hand, the new and normative message from God.

For example, the assumption of male gender superiority is a significant aspect of the historical and cultural context of the biblical passages that seem to discuss homosexuality. Old Testament scholar Martti Nissinen has concluded from his cross-cultural research that "ancient Near Eastern sources in general are concerned with gender roles and their corresponding sexual practices, not with expressing a particular sexual orientation."[49] Thus, generally in the ancient Near East, sexual contact between two men was condemned as a confusion of gender roles. The cultural emphasis on male gender superiority also appears in

Old Testament narratives and laws. Old Testament scholar Phyllis Bird concludes, "In the final analysis it [prohibition of homosexual behavior] is a matter of gender identity and roles, not sexuality."[50] The same attitude is present in the New Testament, reflecting its Greek and Roman cultural context. New Testament scholar Victor Paul Furnish states that Romans 1:26–27 presupposes "that same-sex intercourse compromises what patriarchal societies regard as the properly dominant role of males over females."[51]

When we are engaged in controversy, we need to be patient and tolerant with each other until we better understand the contexts from which the controversial passages have come.

Guideline #7. "Seek to interpret a particular passage of the Bible in light of all the Bible."

Confessional Origin

The Second Helvetic Confession: *"We hold that interpretation of Scripture to be orthodox and genuine which is gleaned from the Scriptures themselves . . . and expounded in the light of like and unlike passages and of many and clearer passages."*[52]

The Westminster Confession: *"The infallible rule of interpretation of Scripture, is the Scripture itself; and therefore, when there is a question about the true and full sense of any scripture (which is not manifold, but one), it may be searched and known by other places that speak more clearly."*[53]

Commentary

In this final guideline we return to where we began. This guideline affirms that there is a central unifying theme in Scripture—creation, fall, and redemption in Jesus Christ. Scripture is not simply an assortment of quotable sayings. It is a story about a real person. It has a saving purpose. We need to interpret the parts by the whole, the complex by the simple, the peripheral by the central.

If we interpret every particular passage in the light of the whole Bible, with its overarching theme of creation, fall, and redemption in Jesus Christ, we will be helped to put the discussion of homosexuality into proper perspective. This guideline echoes the first when it says "keeping Christ in the center aids in evaluating the significance of the problems and controversies that always persist in the vigorous, historical life of the church."[54] When we recognize that all of us, of whatever sexual orientation, are created by God, that we are all fallen sinners, and that we can all be redeemed by the life, death, and resurrection of Jesus Christ, homosexuality will no longer be a divisive issue. Peace and progress will again characterize the church when we stop making exceptions to our fundamental principles and we restore the full rights of membership to all our members.[55]

CONCLUSION

Each of these seven guidelines for biblical interpretation is drawn from our Reformed confessional heritage and has been adopted by the church for use in dealing with controversial issues. They are very similar to the principles of interpretation used in other mainstream denominations. I list them again to reinforce their unity of purpose and approach:

1. Recognize that Jesus Christ, the Redeemer, is the center of Scripture. The redemptive activity of God is central to the entire Scripture. The Old Testament themes of the covenant and the messiah testify to this activity. In the center of the New Testament is Jesus Christ: the Word made flesh, the fulfillment of Israel's messianic hope, and the promise of the Kingdom. It is to Christ that the church witnesses. When interpreting Scripture, keeping Christ in the center aids in evaluating the significance of the problems and controversies that always persist in the vigorous, historical life of the church.

2. Let the focus be on the plain text of Scripture, to the grammatical and historical context, rather than to allegory or subjective fantasy.

3. Depend on the guidance of the Holy Spirit in interpreting and applying God's message.

4. Be guided by the doctrinal consensus of the church, which is the rule of faith.

5. Let all interpretations be in accord with the rule of love, the twofold commandment to love God and to love our neighbor.

6. Remember that interpretation of the Bible requires earnest study in order to establish the best text and to interpret the influence of

the historical and cultural context in which the divine message has come.

7. Seek to interpret a particular passage of the Bible in light of all the Bible.

Interpreting the Bible according to these guidelines from our Reformed heritage provides a more accurate understanding of Scripture that brings us into a closer relationship to God and one another.

In the next chapter, I will examine the handful of texts that are usually used to condemn faithful Christian people who are homosexual. I will be guided by these Reformed rules for interpreting the Bible in times of controversy. Let us see what we discover.

5

What the Bible Says and Doesn't Say about Homosexuality

The Bible is a drama of a good God who created a good world. A tragic fall into sin by the world's people alienated them from God. But God would not leave these people alone. God came into the world in the person of Jesus Christ, whose life, teaching, death, and resurrection overcame alienation and renewed the relationship between God and God's people.

Why do I remind you of what you know so well? The reason is that this perspective is often absent from the current debate about homosexuality in the church. That debate focuses on, at most, eight texts: Genesis 19:1–29; Judges 19:1–30; Leviticus 18:1–30; Leviticus 20:1–27; 1 Corinthians 6:9–17; 1 Timothy 1:3–13; Jude 1–25; and Romans 1. Together they cover a maximum of twelve pages in the Bible. None of these texts is about Jesus, nor do they include any of his words.

New Testament scholar Richard Hays, who teaches at Duke University Divinity School, says, "The Bible hardly ever discusses homosexual behavior. There are perhaps half a dozen references to it in all of scripture. In terms of emphasis, it is a minor concern, in contrast, for example, to economic injustice."[1] Nonetheless, in the debate on homosexuality these texts are often taken out of their linguistic, historical, and cultural context and used to condemn a whole group of people. Only Romans 1 deals with some of the central themes of the Bible. Often those who use Romans 1 to condemn homosexuality insert nonbiblical theories to justify their position in ways that subvert the central message of the text.

Most Christians have been told at one time or another that the Bible condemns all homosexual relationships. That view is simply incorrect. For hundreds of years the Bible has been used inappropriately to oppress people who are homosexual. The eight passages I noted above are pulled out of their biblical context to justify that oppression. However, as we will see, when we apply the best methods of biblical interpretation, as derived from the Reformed confessions and adopted by the church (as discussed in the last chapter), a very different picture emerges. Let us look at those eight passages, using the guidelines for biblical interpretation presented in the last chapter.

THE FIRST SEVEN TEXTS

Sodom and Gomorrah: Genesis 19:1–29
The Rape of the Levite's Concubine: Judges 19:1–30

The Old Testament stories most often cited as opposing homosexuality are (1) God's judgment on the men of Sodom and Gomorrah in Genesis 19:1–29 and (2) the parallel story of the rape of the Levite's concubine in Judges 19:1–30. These texts take us into an ancient Near Eastern world whose values are very different than ours. The central idea in these passages is the sacred obligation of hospitality for travelers (and the ways in which sinful people often violated this sacred obligation). In a desert country, to remain outside at night, exposed to the elements, could mean death.[2]

In both stories, a host invites traveling men into his house. Later an angry mob of townspeople surround the house and demand that the host turn his guests over to them. Foreigners are clearly not welcome, and the implication is that they may be raped or killed.[3] Daniel Helminiak, professor of psychology at the State University of West Georgia, points out that in the ancient world homosexual rape was a traditional way for victors to accentuate the subjection of captive enemies and foes. In that culture, the most humiliating experience for a man was to be treated like a woman, and raping a man was the most violent such treatment.[4] As Dale B. Martin, professor of religion at Duke University, says, "To be penetrated was to be inferior because women were inferior."[5] It is an expression of the "ancient horror of the feminine."[6]

In each of the stories, the host attempts to placate the threatening gangs by offering women of his household for the mob to abuse instead of his male guests. Notice the cultural emphasis on the superiority of men over women. As Old Testament scholar Martti Nissinen of the University of Helsinki notes, the critical issue in the ancient Near East was not sexuality but gender, and it was important that the superior position of men over women be maintained.[7] In that culture, the hosts felt that it was more important to protect male visitors in their house than to protect women, even their own daughters or common-law wife! The hosts do not seem to think of the attackers as primarily homosexual, or they would not offer women for them to abuse.

The best available scholarship shows that these texts have nothing to do with homosexuality as such. C.-L. Seow, professor of Old Testament at Princeton Theological Seminary, points out that the sin of Sodom is mentioned several times elsewhere in the Bible, but never in connection with homosexual acts.[8] In Old Testament references to Sodom, the sins of the city are variously described as greed, injustice, inhospitality, excess wealth, indifference to the poor, and general wickedness.[9] In the New Testament, when Jesus referred to the sin of Sodom, as recorded in Luke 10:12 and Matthew 10:15, he was passing judgment on cities that refused hospitality to his traveling disciples.[10] A focus on the supposed homosexual aspect of the Sodom story comes only later in nonbiblical literature, influenced by Greek philosophy, and also in the Muslim Qur'an.[11]

The Old Testament Laws: Leviticus 18 and 20

Leviticus includes a collection of laws known as the Holiness Code, so named because the dominant idea in Leviticus is God's command: "You shall be holy, for I the LORD your God am holy" (Lev. 19:2). Two texts in this collection of laws are cited by those opposed to homosexuality as explicit prohibitions against homosexuality: Leviticus 18:22 and 20:13.

The Israelites had been slaves in Egypt; they had wandered in the desert, subject to attacks from other tribes, starvation, and infectious diseases. They needed cohesiveness, cleanliness, and order in every aspect of their lives. They wanted to keep pure their manner of worshipping God, who had brought them to this land. They were struggling for their own identity. Failure to form a tightknit community could threaten their long-term survival. They needed a code for living.

In response, they developed a Holiness Code to define their religious, civic, and cultural identity. The Holiness Code's function was to achieve the "holy purity" they sought. Its underlying theme was that they must be separate, different from the Egyptians from whom they had escaped and unmixed with the Canaanites into whose land they had now come. How were they to achieve holy purity?

First, Israel's worship practices had to be different from those of the tribes or nations around them. To be like the Canaanites would make them impure, or "defiled." Phyllis Bird, professor of Old Testament at Garrett-Evangelical Seminary, notes: "Israel is enjoined not to follow the practices of the Canaanites who preceded them in the land. . . . The previous inhabitants, through their 'defiling' actions, caused the land to become defiled so that God punished the land, making it vomit out its inhabitants."[12] In contrast, Israel was to be faithful to God, so that they would prosper on this land.

Second, they could not mix with any other kind of people or adopt alien customs if they were to remain pure. Practically, this meant no intermarriage with non-Israelites. However, the Israelites generalized this aspect of the code to mean no mixing of any kind. Thus the Holiness Code forbids such things as sowing a field "with two kinds of seed" and wearing a garment "made of two different materials" (Lev. 19:19).[13]

Third, male gender superiority had to be maintained. We find in Leviticus that actions undermining male gender superiority incur the death penalty. A child who cursed his parents could be put to death, for such an act threatened the social order in a patriarchal society. Adultery was similarly punishable by death, because it was an unlawful use of a woman, who was a man's property, and therefore jeopardized lines of ownership and inheritance. Engaging in homosexual acts was punishable by death, because a man took a passive role and was penetrated, which was the role assigned to a woman.[14] Victor Paul Furnish, professor of New Testament at Perkins School of Theology, Southern Methodist University, points out that a man penetrated was thus impure.[15] By, in effect, mixing genders, he had crossed a cultural boundary, and that could not be tolerated.[16]

It is against this background that Nissinen, Bird, and others interpret the statement, "You shall not lie with a male as with a woman; it is an abomination" (Lev. 18:22; cf. 20:13).[17] The Hebrew word *toevah*, translated as "abomination," refers here to something that makes a person ritually unclean, such as having intercourse with a woman while she is menstruating.[18] Ritual purity was considered necessary to distinguish the Israelites from their pagan neighbors.

Jesus was concerned with purity of heart. In Matthew 15 he said to a crowd, "Listen and understand: it is not what goes into the mouth that defiles a person, but it is what comes out of the mouth that defiles" (Matt. 15:10–11). Later he explained to his disciples: "What comes out of the mouth proceeds from the heart, and this is what defiles. For out of the heart come evil intentions, murder, adultery, fornication, theft, false witness, slander. These are what defile a person, but to eat with unwashed hands does not defile" (Matt. 15:18–20).

When we see Jesus as the fulfillment of the law (Matt. 5:17), we understand that our challenge is not meticulously to maintain culturally conditioned laws, but rather, with Jesus, to love God and love our neighbor (Matt. 22:36–40). When these texts in Leviticus are taken out of their historical and cultural context and applied to faithful, God-worshipping Christians who are homosexual, it does violence to them. They are being condemned for failing to conform to an ancient culturally conditioned code that is not applicable to them or their circumstances. Even Louisville Presbyterian Seminary New Testament professor Marion Soards, who opposes homosexuality on other grounds, agrees that "it is impossible to declare the necessary relevance of these verses for our world today."[19]

New Testament Vice Lists: 1 Corinthians 6:9, 1 Timothy 1:10

Opponents of equal rights for people who are homosexual also cite a pair of New Testament texts—1 Corinthians 6:9–17, and 1 Timothy 1:3–13—as informing us about homosexuality. What makes these passages distinct is that, in their original Greek, they contain two words, *arsenokoites* and *malakos*, that some scholars argue refer to male homosexual activity.[20] As a result, a disproportionate amount of scholarly attention has been given to these texts and these two words. But to give attention to these two words is to embark on a journey of linguistic technicality. Brian Blount, professor of New Testament at Princeton Theological Seminary, notes that the meaning of these words is not at all clear, and their reference to homosexuality as such has been challenged.[21] Martti Nissinen observes that both words appear in lists of vices that seem to reflect general concerns of Hellenistic Jews about the deplorable state of Greek society.[22]

Arsenokoites and *malakos* both occur in 1 Corinthians 6:9, and *arsenokoites* recurs in 1 Timothy 1:10. Because the words occur in lists with no context, it is difficult to know exactly what they mean. Compounding the situation, Nissinen notes that Paul, in the list he cites, is using *arsenokoites* for the first time ever either in Greek or Jewish literature, thus making it very difficult to interpret.[23]

The debate over the meaning of these words illumines the various methods that scholars use to define terms. Dale Martin disagrees with those who read the two words, *arsen* (male) and *koites* (bed), as one and thereby create a new term for men who have sex with men.[24] Martin objects that "this approach is linguistically invalid," using as an illustration that the English word "understand" has nothing to do with either standing or being under. He articulates an important principle: "The only reliable way to define a word is to analyze its use in as many different contexts as possible."[25] Martin concludes, after analyzing Greek writings both secular and Christian, that *arsenokoites* probably refers to "some kind of economic exploitation, probably by sexual means: rape or sex by economic coercion, prostitution, pimping, or something of the sort."[26] He further asserts that "no one should be allowed to get away with claiming that 'of course' the term refers to 'men who have sex with other men.'"[27]

The term *malakos* is somewhat easier to understand because it is a common word. It literally means "soft" and often connotes effeminacy, which in that culture was treated as a moral failing. Nissinen observes that, in the patriarchal culture of the time, lack of self-control and yielding to pleasures were both considered signs of effeminacy.[28] Contemporary scholars would rightly be embarrassed to invoke effeminacy as a moral category today. Unfortunately, however, as Martin laments, translating biblical terms on the assumption that all homosexual behavior is sinful is not yet embarrassing.[29]

In 1 Timothy 1:10, which many scholars date later than Paul's work, *arsenokoites* appears in a list of vices.[30] The NRSV translates it with the ambiguous word "sodomites." Victor Furnish notes that the word "sodomite" is not used in the Hebrew text of the Old Testament, not even to mean "a resident of Sodom." It was introduced in English in a half dozen Old Testament passages in the King James Version of the Bible in 1611. Nor does the word appear in the Greek text of the New Testament.[31] In 1 Timothy 1:10, "the fact that *arsenokoitai* [the plural of *arsenokoites,* which the NRSV translates as "sodomites"] is followed by slave traders, a group who exploited others, adds weight to Martin's evidence for *arsenokoitai* as sexual exploiters of some sort, since the vices in the lists were often grouped according to their similarity to other vices in the list."[32]

Nissinen argues, "The modern concept of 'homosexuality' should by no means be read into Paul's text, nor can we assume that Paul's words in I Corinthians 6:9 'condemn all homosexual relations' in all times and places and ways. The meanings of the word are too vague to justify this claim, and Paul's words should not be used for generalizations that go beyond his experience and world."[33] Many scholars, such as Marion Soards, believe that "only indirectly may we derive information regarding homosexuality from this material."[34] Once again, careful attention to the linguistic, historical, and cultural context has led to a richer and more nuanced understanding of the plain text.

Jude 5–7

The Letter of Jude consists of only one chapter that runs just over one page and comes right before the book of Revelation. Very few writers pay much attention to this brief and obscure book. Yet New Testament scholar Thomas E. Schmidt, who is director of the Westminster Center in Santa Barbara, California, claims that the book of Jude makes reference to homosexuality.[35]

The Letter of Jude is the only book of the Bible that relates the sin of Sodom and Gomorrah to "sexual immorality." Schmidt, however, makes the broad claim that "The first Christians undoubtedly connected the sin of Sodom to the sin of same-sex relations."[36] The situation is, however, much more complex.

In Genesis 6:1–4 angels ("sons of God") are described as coming down to earth to have sex with human women ("daughters of humans").[37] When Jude 6 refers to "angels who did not keep their own position," it is believed by most scholars that he is referring to events in Genesis 6:1–4. In Genesis 19:1–29 Lot's guests are also described as angels.

Jude 7 draws a parallel between the "unnatural lust" of angels who wanted to have sex with human women (Gen. 6:1–4) and the men of Sodom who wanted to have sex with (male) angels (Gen. 19:1–29).[38] Jude writes that for their transgressions the Lord has kept the angels "in eternal chains in deepest darkness for the judgment of the great day" (v. 6) Likewise, the men of Sodom suffered "a punishment of eternal fire" (v. 7).

As one can see, in Jude there is a lot of discussion about sex between humans and angels (angels with human women, and human men with male angels) that is labeled as "sexual immorality" and "unnatural lust." But for Schmidt, or anyone else, to make the leap that this text somehow condemns present-day Christians who are homosexual strikes me as bizarre. In studying the seven texts that are often cited in opposition to homosexuality, we discover a significant body of scholarship that concludes that these texts have no direct application to faithful, God-loving, twenty-first-century Christians who are homosexual. What is more, this scholarly consensus includes many people who have traditionally opposed equal rights for people who are homosexual, such as scholars Richard Hays and Marion Soards. That leaves just one text, Romans 1.

ROMANS 1

The conflict over the meaning of biblical texts becomes acute when we look at Romans 1. Some conservative scholars who dismiss the relevance of the seven previously discussed texts to the issue of homosexuality argue that Romans 1 is a theological statement that has direct application for our time. I believe, however, that a close and careful look at the text, using the best methods of biblical interpretation, will reveal that Paul is making a statement about idolatry, not sexuality per se, and that Paul's writings also reflect many of the cultural assumptions of his time.

Paul's thesis statement for his letter to the Romans comes in Romans 1, verse 16: "For I am not ashamed of the gospel; it is the power of God for salvation to everyone who has faith, to the Jew first and also to the Greek." The very next sentence states that thesis in another way: "The one who is righteous will live by faith" (Rom. 1:17). No one is excluded from the possibility of receiving God's salvation. The gospel that Paul is proclaiming in Romans does not center on the issue of sexuality. It focuses on the universality of sin and the free grace of salvation through the life, death, and resurrection of Jesus Christ. That is the essence of the Christian message.

Idolatry, Not Sexuality

In Romans 1:18–32, Paul is writing about idolatry, that is worshipping, giving our ultimate allegiance, to anything in the creation instead of God, the Creator.[39] Paul is writing from Corinth, a bustling seaport town that was "notorious for vice of all kinds." Apparently, in the

Roman Empire a common name for a prostitute was "a Corinthian girl."[40] Paul writes of people worshipping "images resembling a mortal human being or birds or four-footed animals or reptiles" (v. 23)—instead of God. Paul concluded that because the Corinthians engaged in idolatry, "God gave them up to degrading passions" (v. 26).

It seems as though Paul is setting up his Jewish readers. It is easy at this point in the text for them, and for us, to feel self-righteous. Jews didn't worship images of birds or animals or reptiles. Those were typical Gentile sins. But then Paul lowers the boom on his readers by listing other sins that proceed from idolatry—covetousness, malice, envy, strife, deceit, craftiness, gossip, slander. Idolaters could become haughty, boastful, rebellious toward parents, foolish, faithless, heartless, ruthless. Now Paul is talking to all of us, speaking to those sins of attitude to which we sometimes succumb when we turn our ultimate allegiance away from the true God.

Paul makes this point again, in Romans 2:1. We are without excuse, especially when we judge others. Why? Because in God's sight we are all given to idolatry. Paul is driving home the point that is at the heart of Reformation theology: no one is righteous before God. Paul has been criticizing those idolatrous Corinthian Gentiles. Now he is saying to his Jewish colleagues, and to us, no one is righteous. We are all sinners. That is Paul's point in Romans 1.

Cultural Norms, Not a Theology of Creation

What does Paul mean by "natural" and "unnatural" in Romans 1:26–27? In the original Greek, the words are *physis*, "nature," and *para physin*, "against nature."[41]

For Paul, "unnatural," is a synonym for "unconventional."[42] It means something surprisingly out of the ordinary. The most significant evidence that "natural" meant "conventional" is that God acted "contrary to nature" (Rom. 11:13–24). That is, God did something very unusual by pruning the Gentiles from a wild olive tree, where they grew in their natural state, and grafting them into the cultivated olive tree of God's people (Rom. 11:24). Since it cannot be that God sinned, to say that God did what is "contrary to nature" or "against nature" (v. 24) means that God did something surprising and out of the ordinary.[43]

Paul is not talking in Romans 1:26–27 about a violation of the order of creation. In Paul's vocabulary, *physis* (nature) is not a synonym for *ktisis* (creation). In speaking about what is "natural," Paul is merely accepting the conventional view of people and how they ought to behave in first-century Hellenistic-Jewish culture.[44]

Male Gender Dominance

The theme of male gender dominance appears again and again in the texts that many claim deal with homosexuality, including Romans 1. Both the Hebrew and the Greek cultures were patriarchal. Men were, and intended to remain, dominant over women. Paul assumes the conventions of these cultures that he is addressing. He uses terms familiar in the Greek-speaking synagogues such as "impurity" (1:24) and "shameless" (1:27), which are part of the Jewish language of purity. And he is equally familiar with terms that are rooted in Greek Stoic philosophy, such as "lusts" (1:24) and "passions" (1:26) that denote erotic passion and uncontrolled desire.[45]

In Romans 1:26, Paul writes: "Their women exchanged natural intercourse for unnatural." As Nissinen notes, the phrase "their women" is a clear indication of a gender role structure.[46] But, he contends, "Paul's understanding of the naturalness of men's and women's gender roles is not a matter of genital formation and their functional purpose, which today is considered by many the main criterion for the natural and unnatural."[47] Rather, in the culture Paul is addressing, a man and a woman each had a designated place and role in society, which could not be exchanged. For example, Paul in 1 Corinthians 11:3–16 outlines a strict hierarchical ladder of God-Christ-man-woman. Strict gender role differences are set out, manifested by different hairstyles. Paul asks, "Does not nature itself teach you that if a man wears long hair, it is degrading to him, but if a woman has long hair, it is her glory?" (1 Cor. 11:14). In that culture, to violate these roles would be a matter of shame before God.[48]

For Paul, transgressions of gender role boundaries cause "impurity," a violation of the Jewish purity code (1:24).[49] Nissinen explains that it is women taking the man's active role in sex that was seen as "unnatural."[50] The text does not say that women had sex with other women. They could have been condemned for taking the dominant position in heterosexual intercourse, or for engaging in nonprocreative sexual acts with male partners.[51] The issue is gender dominance, and in that culture women were to be passive and not active in sexual matters.

Control and Moderation in All Things

In Hebrew culture and in Stoic philosophy (which was influential in the Roman Empire, particularly in Greece, during Paul's time) control and moderation in all things were highly valued, especially regarding emotion and sexuality. Going to excess, whether eating too much, sleeping too much, or giving in to excessive passion of any kind was viewed as a moral failing.[52] The goal was to make correct "use" of all things. The "natural use" of sex was to be very controlled, avoiding passion.[53] Paul in Romans 1:26–27 would be rightly understood to be talking not about wrongly oriented desires, but about inordinate desires—going to excess, losing control.[54] Idolaters fail to give God glory and gratitude. God then allows them to lose control in erotic passion, which brings them dishonor.[55]

The Plain Text

Those who are opposed to equal rights for Christian gay and lesbian people make several serious errors in interpreting Romans 1: (1) they lose sight of the fact that this passage is primarily about idolatry, (2) they overlook Paul's point that we are all sinners, (3) they miss the cultural subtext, and (4) they apply Paul's condemnation of immoral sexual activity to faithful gay and lesbian Christians who are not idolaters, who love God, and who seek to live in thankful obedience to God.

Heterosexual sex can be either moral or immoral, depending on its context. The same is true of homosexual sex. If Paul walked into a party at the Playboy Mansion today or observed college students "hooking up" at a fraternity party, he would be appalled and rightly condemn the activities going on there. But no one would conclude from that observation that Paul had ruled out all heterosexual sex as immoral. Everyone would understand that Paul was not talking about married Christian heterosexual couples who love God and seek to follow Jesus.

Paul's condemnation of immoral sexual behavior is not appropriately applied to contemporary gay or lesbian Christians who are not idolaters, who love God, and who seek to live in thankful obedience to God. I think Jeffrey Siker, professor of New Testament at Loyola Marymount University, says it best: "We know of gay and lesbian Christians who truly worship and serve the one true God and yet still affirm in positive ways their identity as gay and lesbian people. Paul apparently knew of no homosexual Christians. We do."[56]

NONBIBLICAL THEORIES IMPOSED UPON ROMANS 1

Those who oppose homosexuality claim that they are appealing to Romans 1. Upon closer examination, it is clear that many are imposing their own nonbiblical theories on the Pauline text. The most common additions to the plain text of Romans 1 are (1) appeals to natural law and (2) the assumption that Genesis somehow contains a prescription for heterosexual, monogamous marriage. These are *not* necessary to understand Paul's basic point in Romans 1 that all are sinners and are saved by grace through faith in Christ. Let us examine these theories that are imported into Romans 1, and other texts, in an attempt to justify the condemnation of all contemporary homosexuality. A number of subissues under natural law and heterosexual marriage may seem out of place in a discussion of Romans 1, but I present them here because they are assumptions that, when brought to Romans 1, distort the interpretation of Paul's message.

Natural Law

One argument made by conservative interpreters is that we can be guided by a nonbiblical standard, natural law. Natural law is composed of those unquestioned assumptions that most people in the culture accept. Ralph McInerny at the University of Notre Dame defines natural law as "the claim that there are certain judgments we have already made and could not help making."[57] The problem is that this could also be a good definition for prejudice.[58]

The unreflective appeal to nature is exemplified by a remark of fundamentalist minister Jerry Falwell. On *Meet the Press* following the November 2004 presidential election, Falwell, pushing his priorities for President Bush's second term, said, "I think it's unthinkable that we're debating what a family is, a man married to a woman. They've got that right in the barnyard." In his colorful manner of speaking, Falwell appealed to what, to him, was obvious in nature—animals have sexual relations, male with female.[59] That model of nature is an often-used appeal to natural law.

As it turns out, however, not all animals are heterosexual. Biologist Bruce Bagemihl has documented homosexual relations in 450 different species in the animal world. Same-sex behavior includes not only copulation, but courtship and parental activities.[60] I am not arguing here that we should base our understanding of sex on animal behavior, but, rather, pointing out that those who do, citing male-female relations as universal in nature, are in error.

As we saw in chapter 2 in the discussion of Scottish Common Sense philosophy, theologians often appeal to natural law in an attempt to argue divine sanction for their cultural assumptions. A classic example of the misuse of natural law in theology is Robert Gagnon's *The Bible and Homosexual Practice: Texts and Hermeneutics.*[61] Gagnon is a professor of New Testament at Pittsburgh Theological Seminary. His book is acclaimed by some opponents of gay and lesbian equality as the definitive biblical word on homosexuality.

The irony is that Gagnon doesn't seem to need the Bible because, he argues, everything the Bible says about homosexuality comes initially from the observation of nature. In fact, in the conclusion to his book, Gagnon actually says what many heterosexual people believe: "Acceptance of biblical revelation is thus not a prerequisite for rejecting the legitimacy of same-sex intercourse."[62] So where does he believe the constraints against homosexual behavior are found? As it turns out, behind all of the ancient sources, including biblical sources, according to Gagnon, is "the simple recognition of a 'fittedness' of the sex organs, male to female."[63] He goes on to say that the Old Testament Holiness Code "was responding to the conviction that same-sex intercourse was fundamentally incompatible with the creation of men and women as anatomically complementary sexual beings."[64] He also refers to "Paul's own reasoning, grounded in divinely-given clues in nature."[65] In each of these statements, Gagnon gives priority to nature over revelation.

According to Gagnon, pagans, as well as Jews and Christians, find "the material creation around human beings and the bodily design of humans themselves, guiding us into the truth about the nature of God and the nature of human sexuality respectively."[66]

The contemporary appeal to natural law, by Gagnon and others, has a function similar to Scottish Common Sense philosophy in an earlier era. Both contend that the truth is obvious. Both rely heavily on sensory evidence. Both assume that no interpretation is needed. Both therefore assert common human prejudices as self-evident truths. Giving priority to natural law opens the door to bring in all manner of assumptions and prejudices that have nothing to do with the biblical text. Let's take a close look at some of Gagnon's assumptions.

1. Sexual Orientation: A Choice?

Relying on his inaccurate assumptions about what is "natural" Gagnon claims, "Certainly no one is born a homosexual."[67] Clearly there is no biblical warrant for this statement. In fact, Jesus, immediately after his teaching on divorce and his recommendation of marriage, states that some people are born eunuchs (Matt. 19:10–12). In the NEB these people are described as "incapable of marriage" (Matt. 19:12). In ancient time, there were no doubt people who were incapable of heterosexual sexual activity and thus were considered "eunuchs." Old Testament scholar Martti Nissinen suggests that in our contemporary context those who are eunuchs from their mother's wombs might well include homosexuals, because they simply lack sexual desire for people of the opposite sex.[68]

There is also no scientific warrant for Gagnon's claim. In a comprehensive review of the literature on the subject of sexual orientation, David G. Myers, professor of psychology at Hope College, observes that based on all the available evidence, most psychologists "view sexual orientation as neither willfully chosen nor willfully changed."[69] I will discuss this more fully in chapter 6.

2. Can People Who Are Homosexual Become Heterosexual?

Having asserted that no one is homosexual by nature, Gagnon claims that all people who are homosexual have willfully chosen that behavior and therefore can successfully change their sexual identity. Once again there is no biblical or scientific warrant for that position. When all of the studies and the testimony have been sifted, it is apparent that when people claim that lesbian and gay people can change, they are almost always referring to behavior and not orientation. In fact, when you probe beyond the assertions, Gagnon acknowledges that "therapists define *success* as management of unwanted desires, not complete elimination."[70] Thomas Schmidt, who supports traditional limits on homosexuals in the church, concludes: "As numerous books by ministry leaders show, their focus is on changed behavior, they are honest about the probability of ongoing temptation."[71] Even Andrew Comiskey, a prominent "ex-gay," agrees. He uses two friends, Karen and Jim, to illustrate his point. He says of them, "Neither can choose not to have homosexual feelings anymore than heterosexuals can deny their impulse for the opposite sex."[72]

By acknowledging that "reparative" or "conversion" therapy is addressing only behavior rather than orientation, opponents of homosexuality are actually admitting that, in fact, sexual orientation is a part of someone's nature and may be just as God-given as heterosexuality. David Myers, in his review of the scientific literature on sexual orientation, concludes, "Sexual orientation is like handedness: Most people are one way, some are the other. A very few are truly ambidextrous. Regardless, the way one is endures."[73]

When people who are homosexual are able to accept their orientation, it frees them to find a loving partner of their own sex and experience the joy of companionship, just as heterosexuals do in a marriage. The church should celebrate such unions, rather than imposing unbiblical and unscientific assumptions upon this group of people.

3. Is Homosexuality Idolatry?

Since Gagnon claims, in spite of all the evidence to the contrary, that homosexuality is a willful choice, he then proceeds to *define* same-sex intercourse *as* idolatry.[74] His definition makes sense only if you *start* with the *assumption* that homosexuality is sinful. If, on the other hand, you start with the question of whether people who are homosexual are idolatrous, you could simply speak with real Christian people who are gay and lesbian and quickly discover that in fact they love Jesus and seek to serve God. The debate would be over.

Gagnon does not deal with how real Christian gay and lesbian people express their love for each other or their love for God. He does not acknowledge the devout Christian people who are living in faithful, monogamous same-sex unions. Instead, he has created his own theoretical model of idolatrous sex and then claims that it applies to all people who are homosexual.

Moreover, Gagnon does not demonstrate that the immoral sexual relations Paul condemns are related to the love of contemporary faithful gay and lesbian Christians. He simply asserts it. The lives of Christian people who are homosexual refute Gagnon's assertions. If one takes the time to know real Christian people who are homosexual, one finds that their love is not any more lustful than that of people who are heterosexual, nor is it motivated by idolatry.

Jesus dealt with real people in the midst of their daily lives. He didn't start with culturally biased assumptions and then use them as a club to punish those who were not like him. Rather, he went to the people and helped them develop a closer relationship with God. If we start with Jesus and seek to follow him, we will then be guided to deal with real people and endeavor to help everyone know and serve God.

4. Homosexual Relationships: The Worst Sin of All?

The conclusion of Gagnon's chain of reasoning, based on his appeal to natural law, is twofold: (1) lesbian and gay sexual relations are sinful as such; and (2) they are the worst sin of all. Gagnon declares that, on the basis of observation of nature, we can know that all same-sex intercourse is the "road that leads to death: physically, morally, and spiritually."[75] He simply asserts, with no supporting evidence, that sexual relations between contemporary Christian people who are homosexual are sinful as such.

Secondly, he argues, "we all sin but not all sin is equally offensive to God and not all sin is to be treated in the same way."[76] In fact, however, that is the exact opposite of what Paul argues in Romans 1:29–32! Paul declares that *all* of the sins that he lists, not just immoral sexual relations, are worthy of death. Gagnon may choose to take a position in opposition to Paul, but he cannot claim to be biblical in doing so.

Given Gagnon's assumption that homosexual behavior will cause a person to be excluded from the kingdom of God, it seems reasonable then to conclude that, for him, a prerequisite to salvation is to imitate heterosexual behavior or be celibate. That would of course contradict Paul's view that all are sinners, that no one is saved by works, and that all can be saved by God's grace.

Homosexuality an Example of the Fallenness of Humanity?

Richard Hays, writing on New Testament sexual ethics, takes a mediating, yet conservative, position on the consequences of God's judgment in Romans. He writes, "Paul is not describing the individual life histories of pagan sinners; not every pagan has first known the true God of Israel and then chosen to turn away into idolatry. When Paul writes: 'they exchanged the truth about God for a lie,' he is giving a global account of the universal fall of humanity."[77] Hays then asserts that "Paul singles out homosexual intercourse for special attention because he regards it as providing a particularly graphic image of the way in which human fallenness distorts God's created order."[78]

One of the problems with this argument is that either humanity's fall is universal or it is not. You cannot argue that everyone is fallen (the essential Christian message) and then go on to single out particular groups of people as extrafallen. Furthermore, like Gagnon, Hays is making huge assumptions about what God intended to create. As I have already shown, examples from the animal kingdom seem to show that God pretty clearly did intend to create homosexual animals. Furthermore, the best scientific evidence also seems to show a genetic influence on sexual orientation, as well as biological differences between homosexual and heterosexual people. This data would suggest that homosexuality is indeed part of God's created order.[79]

For Hays, God's "created order" includes a prescription for heterosexual marriage as the only acceptable context for sexual intercourse. He declares, "Marriage between man and woman is the normative form for human sexual fulfillment, and homosexuality is one among the many tragic signs that we are a broken people, alienated from God's loving purpose."[80] Again, by singling out a particular group of people, Hays is contradicting the essential Christian message that we are *all* broken people, saved through the life, death, and resurrection of Jesus Christ. Furthermore, while I too believe that monogamous marriage is the best context for human sexual fulfillment, as I will show in the following section, there is no particular scriptural warrant for monogamous *heterosexual* marriage as the norm for all people.[81]

A Model of Monogamous Heterosexual Marriage in Genesis?

Many who would like to use Romans 1 to oppose equal rights for people who are homosexual ground their position in the creation accounts in Genesis 1–2. The argument goes something like this: homosexual relations are against nature, because they are contrary to the pattern placed within creation.[82] What is that pattern? According to some, like Thomas Schmidt, it is monogamous, heterosexual, marriage.[83] However, Genesis 1–2 contains no reference to homosexuality or marriage. These chapters were not written to answer the questions that are now being put to them.

As Old Testament scholar Phyllis Bird notes, the laws and traditions that regulated sexual relations and marriage in ancient Israel *never* referred to the creation texts as models.[84] Genesis 1, she argues, actually describes how humans are like and unlike God. People are made in God's image and likeness, so they are separate from and superior to other animals. But in their sexuality, they are identified as male and female, not as husband and wife, or even man and woman. Victor Furnish further reminds us that in contrast to all of the ancient Near Eastern deities, Israel's God was regarded as *asexual*.[85] Thus in their sexuality, humankind is *like* every other created species and *unlike* God.[86]

Indeed, Furnish asserts that Genesis 2:23–25 "neither commands nor presumes a 'monogamous' relationship between man and woman and . . . it offers no comment on 'marriage' as such."[87] Moreover, Old Testament heroes of the faith certainly did *not* model monogamy, but rather followed the patterns of their culture, with multiple wives, concubines, and slaves as sexual partners. The Bible not only approves, but appears to mandate such behavior. However, as Furnish notes, the prescription to "be fruitful and multiply" cannot mean that everyone must marry and reproduce, for the creation stories "take no account whatever of the physically or mentally impaired, the celibate, the impotent—or of those who in modern times have come to be described as 'homosexual.'"[88]

This notion that a model of monogamous, heterosexual marriage is somehow contained in Genesis 1 is simply not true. It appears to be an artificial construct designed to deny the rights of marriage to those who are homosexual. As David Balch, professor of New Testament at Brite Divinity School, observes, where a theology of creation is stressed, as by those opposed to equality for gays and lesbians, "subordination and submission are usually emphasized."[89] On the other hand, where a theology of redemption, such as Paul offers in Romans 3, is stressed, "freedom, mutuality, and equality are usually emphasized."[90]

I think that the contemporary model of Christian marriage is a good one for heterosexual people: one man and one woman should marry for life and, if they choose, bear and care for children. This model is not found in Genesis, however. Moreover, it took Western society many centuries to come to it,[91] and even so, half of the heterosexual people in American society do not follow it. On the other hand, many Christian gay and lesbian people have committed themselves to one lifelong partner. Many care for children, and some that I know have adopted children with special needs. They seem to have gotten the point of the contemporary Christian model of marriage and are living it out.

Reuniting the Binary Split?

An extreme version of the notion that salvation is found only in the uniting of male and female is found in Robert Gagnon's work. He renders the Genesis story in this way:

> In Gen. 2:18–24, a binary or sexually undifferentiated human (the *adam*) is split into two sexually differentiated beings. Marriage is treated by the Yahwist as a reunion of the sexual unity of the original *adam*. One can no more dismiss the story's implicit relevance for

proscriptions of same-sex intercourse than one can dismiss its perti-
nence for attitudes against bestiality (cf. 2:20). . . . Two males or two
females in sexual union would not equal an originally binary being
or sexual whole.[92]

Interestingly, in Plato's *Symposium* a similar myth of an original
whole being divided is presented by an intoxicated Aristophanes. Originally there were three kinds of beings, a male, a female, and an androg-
ynon that shared equally in the male and female. Zeus sliced these
beings in half and each searched for its counterpart in order to become
whole again by having sexual relations. The androgynous, of course,
would be heterosexual, the male half searching to be reunited with the
female half. Aristophanes observes, "Our adulterers are mostly descended
from that sex, whence likewise are derived our man-courting women
and adulteresses."[93] It's a curious theory, but once again, there is simply
no biblical warrant for that position.

The Male-Female Relationship as the Image of God in Humanity?

The Presbyterian Confession of 1967, which was influenced by the theological method of Karl Barth (see the discussion of neo-orthodoxy in
chapter 3), became a significant source in the struggle to overcome prejudice against people of color and, by analogy, women.[94] Yet in 1978 the
United Presbyterian Task Force on Homosexuality noted Barth's opposition to full equality for gay and lesbian people.[95] Unfortunately, Barth,
like many others, made an exception to his usual method of interpreting
Scripture when it came to the issue of gender and homosexuality.

Appealing to his interpretation of natural law and the false assumption that there is a model for heterosexual marriage in Genesis, Barth
wrote, "Man is directed to woman and woman to man . . . this mutual
orientation constitutes the being of each."[96] According to Barth's view,
being fully human is known only in the male-female relationship, and
the marriage relationship is the fullest expression of the image of God
in human beings.[97]

Like others who rely on natural law, Barth was biased in favor of the
male gender. According to Barth, in the marriage relationship, the husband reflects Jesus and the wife reflects the Christian community. "She
is," Barth wrote, "subordinated to her husband as the whole community is to Christ."[98]

In his analysis, Barth engaged in the sort of natural theology he usually condemned by appealing to what he referred to as "a little knowledge

of life."[99] By making an argument on the basis of what he considered "natural," Barth departed from the biblical text and instead inserted his own culturally conditioned opinions. As Elouise Renich Fraser, professor of theology and dean at Palmer Theological Seminary, comments: "By making marriage the epitome of co-humanity, Barth places some human relationships automatically under suspicion, excludes some human beings from the possibility of full humanity, and reinforces old stereotypes of male and female, thus failing to help his readers hear the old story with new ears."[100] Barth's firm commitment to male gender superiority causes him to reject all homosexual relationships.[101]

Today many Protestants repeat Barth's assertion that monogamous, heterosexual marriage is the exemplification of the image of God in humanity and use that to oppose full membership in the church for people who are homosexual. Barth's view has also become one basis for attempts to change people who are homosexual into people who are heterosexual. For example, "ex-gay" Andrew Comiskey echoes Barth when he claims, "God also tells us that to discover our true humanity, we must be known by the opposite sex. A fundamental part of our bearing the divine image is its heterosexual reflection. God created man in His image as 'male and female' (Gen. 1:26–27)."[102] It sounds very much as if Comiskey is saying that we have to engage in heterosexual sex in order to be fully human, which would be a breathtaking misinterpretation of Paul's message in Romans 1.

The claim that the image of God is rooted in the male-female relationship leads us away from the biblical text. When I was on the task force on homosexuality at Pasadena Presbyterian Church, one of our members, a former missionary with a PhD in New Testament, argued in favor of the Barthian view that a person was not fully human unless in a heterosexual marriage. His argument offended various committee members, including a never-married woman who was a former missionary. Our one gay member quietly said, "That sure makes it hard on Jesus."

Biblically Jesus Christ *is* the image of God (Col.1:15; 2 Cor. 4:4). But the image of God in Jesus was not a consequence of some unique human attribute, like maleness or marital status. It was rather the result of his reflecting the love of God fully in his life. We human beings reflect God's love only sporadically and partially, whereas Jesus showed us God's love consistently and wholly.

The gospel, the good news, is that all people can have a relationship with God through Jesus Christ. We reflect Christ's presence in our lives by showing love for God and each other. Thus, the image of God is not a capacity embodied only in some classes of people but denied to others. To be in God's image is possible for all—black and white, male and female, gay and straight, married and unmarried.

We need to return to a biblical understanding of God, creation, sin, salvation, and love. Those who rely instead on natural law and biased cultural assumptions twist and distort the fundamental message of the gospel.

There are around 3,000 verses in the Bible that express God's concern for the poor and oppressed.[103] In contrast, there is a tiny handful of verses that some people claim condemn homosexuality. None of them, properly interpreted, refers to contemporary Christian people who are homosexual.

A RELEVANT BIBLICAL ANALOGY

The acceptance of people who are homosexual is grounded in the central message of Scripture as interpreted through the lens of Jesus' life and ministry. In addition, there are specific biblical passages that show the church changing its mind and accepting people who previously were considered unclean and unacceptable. Perhaps the most instructive is the long narrative in Acts 10–15 that records how the church opened itself to receive Gentiles on whom God's Spirit had fallen, without requiring them to behave like Jews.

That narrative culminates in Acts 15, at a gathering that is usually referred to as the Council of Jerusalem. (I sometimes ask Presbyterians to think of it as their first General Assembly.) Certain individuals from the "sect of the Pharisees" resisted the new reality and insisted that in order to be saved, it was necessary for men to be circumcised and all people to keep the law of Moses (Acts 15:5).

However, both Peter and Paul had admitted Gentiles to the church solely on the basis that the Holy Spirit had been given to these non-Jews. These Gentiles did not have to meet any of the former Jewish requirements. Indeed, Peter challenged the church leaders in Jerusalem: "Now therefore why are you putting God to the test by placing on the neck of the disciples a yoke that neither our ancestors nor we have been able to bear?" (Acts 15:10).

So the council members listened to testimony by Peter and then by Paul and Barnabas. Peter recounted a vision that came to him when he was in a trance. God gave him a new revelation, that there were no clean and unclean people in God's sight. Gentiles were not unclean as a class and thus were not to be excluded from full participation in the church. Peter said, "God, who knows the human heart, testified to them by giving them the Holy Spirit, just as he did to us; and in cleansing their hearts by faith he has made no distinction between them and us" (Acts 15:8–9). Paul and Barnabas told of signs and wonders that God had done among the Gentiles. God was doing a new thing.

After hearing the testimony of those who had been working among the Gentiles, James gave an authoritative interpretation. He gave weight to the words of Peter, "we will be saved through the grace of the Lord Jesus, just as they will" (15:11). He saw a continuity of the new reality with biblical Judaism. James interpreted the prophet Amos (9:11–12) to say that God had always purposed the conversion of the Gentiles. Now the church had experienced what God had planned.[104]

Luke Timothy Johnson, professor of New Testament at Chandler School of Theology, Emory University, challenges us, "Remember please, the stakes: The Gentiles were 'by nature' unclean, and were 'by practice' polluted by idolatry. . . . The decision to let the Gentiles in 'as such' . . . came into direct conflict with the accepted interpretation of Torah and what God wanted of humans."[105] Johnson thus affirms that the question of accepting people who are homosexual as full members of the church "is analogous to the one facing earliest Christianity after Gentiles started being converted."[106] New Testament scholar Jeffrey Siker, accepting that analogy, gives his testimony: "Just as Peter's experience of Cornelius in Acts 10 led him to realize that even Gentiles were receiving God's Spirit, so my experience of various gay and lesbian Christians led me to realize that these Christians have received God's Spirit as gays and lesbians and that the reception of the Spirit has nothing to do with sexual orientation."[107]

In the next chapter we will interact, not with theoretical stereotypes, but with real people who are homosexual. These real people evidence a commitment to Jesus Christ, in spite of continuing persecution from society and the misguided policies of many Christian churches. The Christians who are homosexual whom I know show a profound love for Jesus and a deep commitment to marriage and the care of children.

Let's get to know them.

6

Real People and Real Marriage

Moving beyond Stereotypes and Coded Language

Jesus dealt with real people in the midst of their daily struggles. Too often in the church today, however, our debates are filled with stereotypes, abstract theories, and caricatures of people who are homosexual. Careless use of language distorts our perception of real people. Take, for instance, the pejorative phrase "the gay lifestyle." For many people it is a code that calls up images of promiscuity, bizarre behavior in gay pride parades, and the specter of AIDS. The stereotype of the "gay lifestyle" is just not applicable to all LGBT people and certainly not to the devout, Christian, homosexual people who are faithful members of our churches and who simply desire the full rights of membership. I would certainly resent it if people spoke of the "heterosexual lifestyle" and used Howard Stern and Hugh Hefner as the models for all heterosexual men.

I have also, on more than one occasion, been told what I call "The Dirty Little Secret." A heterosexual person, during a discussion of homosexuality, will lower his voice, as if telling me a private confidence. Then he will say something like, "You know *these people* are incapable of maintaining a faithful, monogamous relationship. They are inherently promiscuous." Yet comparative studies of gay couples and heterosexual couples show virtually no difference in the stability of their relationships.[1]

A lifestyle is something that people choose. There are probably as many different lifestyles as there are people. A sexual orientation is not a lifestyle. Almost all gay and lesbian people will tell you that they did not choose their sexual orientation.[2] They just discovered that they were sexually attracted to members of their own sex, usually as early as young people begin to experience sexual attraction. It is convenient for some people who are heterosexual to embrace the theory that homosexuality is a chosen "lifestyle."[3] They can then blame people who are homosexual for being who they are and not deal with the reality of people in their midst who are created differently.[4]

As a church we deplore promiscuity among gay and lesbian people, while at the same time denying the right to marry to those who want to form stable families with the supportive recognition of the Christian community. When I was at Fuller Seminary, I counseled a Missouri-Synod Lutheran student who trusted me with the knowledge that he was gay. His theology condemned him. He had tried to change and tried to be celibate, but once in a while he just couldn't stand it, and he would go to a gay bar in search of a one-night stand. I tried to help him deal with the conflict between his sexual orientation and his conservative theology. I gave him lots of material to read. I shared different theological perspectives with him, in the hope that he could find a way to live with himself. None of it worked. He dropped out of seminary, and from time to time I would get a recommendation form as he was applying for a job, usually as a language teacher. The apostle Paul's and the Reformer Calvin's assumptions that a central reason for marriage was to provide an alternative to promiscuity should certainly apply in this kind of situation.[5] Most people who are heterosexual would not be very successful living a celibate life if that was simply assigned to them by society when they had no such calling from God.[6] The wonder is that so many lesbian and gay people have formed long-term monogamous partnerships, despite all of the barriers that society puts in their way.

Clergy Sexual Misconduct

It is ironic that as the church attempts to identify a biblical standard of sexual morality to apply to people who are homosexual, it has not adequately confronted the issue of clergy sexual misconduct, which is currently epidemic in the church. Priests and Protestant pastors have a tremendous amount of power and influence within their congregations and communities. Unfortunately, many have chosen to abuse that power. The Roman Catholic Church is facing an institutional crisis because of thousands of cases in which adult priests abused their power and privilege to have sex with young parishioners.[7]

The Presbyterian Church, like many Protestant denominations, is plagued by widespread sexual misconduct by pastors (primarily married men who have sexual affairs with women in their congregations).[8] The denomination has taken significant steps to make clear the unacceptability of such behavior and to speed the reporting of it. However, currently, in the Presbyterian Church, these heterosexual male pastors who have clearly violated the teaching of Scripture, their marriage vows, and their ordination vows, by having affairs with female parishioners, are usually treated as individuals, with restoration always a possibility. But in the case of homosexual people the church makes a blanket law a priori that none of them is worthy of ordination to serve as deacon, elder, or minister of Word and Sacrament.

The Evolution of the Purpose of Marriage

The issue of ordaining people who are gay and lesbian is inextricably linked to the issue of marriage. In the Presbyterian Church, as in most Protestant denominations, candidates for ministry are expected either to be married or to remain celibate. However, because gay and lesbian people are currently barred from marriage by the church, gay and lesbian candidates for ministry are never given the option of expressing their sexuality within the bonds of marriage. Instead they are told that they must remain celibate if they hope to be ordained. It's clearly a double standard. The only fair and equitable solution is that *all* people should be expected either to be married or to be celibate.

The church's present policy of excluding a certain class of people from the rights and benefits of marriage echoes many of the now-discredited policies of the past. The Westminster Confession of Faith, for example, which was the sole doctrinal standard of Presbyterianism for more than 300 years, declared that a valid marriage was between Protestants only: "Such as profess the true reformed Religion, should not marry with infidels, papists or other idolaters."[9] By the 1930s, however, Presbyterians began to challenge this ban on marrying Roman Catholics, arguing that "many Roman Catholics are sincere and intelligent believers in our Lord Jesus Christ."[10] Presbyterians later amended the Westminster Confession to remove offending statements against Roman Catholics, including the statement that the pope was the antichrist.[11]

Marriage between the races followed a similar path. In 1948, the California Supreme Court became the first state high court to overturn a law barring marriage between people of different races. At that time, forty of the then-forty-eight states banned interracial marriage.[12] The notion that marriage was only for people of the same race had been a deeply ingrained bias in American society and in the churches. The California Supreme Court decision to permit interracial marriage was controversial in its time.[13] But we have changed our minds, and our laws, for the better.

Marriage has also been defined in such a way as to limit women's civil and human rights. Even in the early twentieth century, in many states women could not own property; if a married woman inherited money from her family, it became the property of her husband. Women were not allowed to vote in national elections until 1920, and opportunities in higher education were limited. The normal state for women was to marry and bear children. They were to be silent partners, leaving all public functions to their husbands.[14]

Over time the Presbyterian Church has also changed its view of the purpose of marriage. Into the 1930s the denomination defined the primary purposes of marriage as bearing children, creating a family, and supporting stability in society. Although in 1930 the Presbyterian Church allowed women to become elders, in that same year a major report on marriage to the General Assembly insisted that motherhood was the proper goal for women. The report encouraged colleges to give more attention to "the science of homemaking" and expressed concern about the use of contraceptives, since the purpose of marriage was procreation.[15] When in 1931 a committee of the Federal Council of Churches recommended that parents consider using artificial means of birth control, the southern Presbyterian Church (PCUS) in indignation withdrew from the council. The northern Presbyterian Church (PCUSA) remained a member but advised the council to "hold its peace on questions of delicacy and morality."

By 1960, however, Presbyterians had adopted the position that the primary purpose of marriage was for the mutual comfort, encouragement, and support of the persons involved. Therefore birth control was appropriate. In 1960 the larger Presbyterian denominations, north and south, issued a joint statement approving of birth control.[16]

Male Gender Superiority and Opposition to Same-Sex Marriage

Recent legal efforts to limit the civil benefits of marriage to heterosexual couples are grounded in the older view that the primary purpose of marriage is procreation. In a Vermont case regarding the rights of homosexual couples, for example, the Vermont assistant attorney general, Eve Jacobs-Carnahan, defended limiting the right of marriage to heterosexual couples by arguing that the purpose of marriage was biological procreation.[17]

In March 2000, Californians approved Proposition 22, the "Defense of Marriage Act," which stipulated that "only marriage between a man and a woman is valid or recognized in California." The groups that pushed hardest for passage of the California act were the Mormon Church and the Roman Catholic Church. The Mormon Church was alleged to have contributed 40 percent of the funds toward marriage-limitation initiatives in other states in the 1990s.[18] Both the Mormons and the Roman Catholics still deny women full participation in the life of their churches. The primary purpose of marriage for them is still for women to bear and care for children, while men exercise public leadership. They have a vested interest in defining marriage in such a way as to maintain their limited and limiting vision.[19]

As we have discussed, there is a strong link between opposition to equality between men and women and opposition to homosexuality.[20] Many religious conservatives view a patriarchal family structure as the key to the health of the church and the nation.[21] In this view, patriarchy, patriotism, and Christianity are woven together into one flag that is flown over all discussions of homosexuality. Homosexuality and women's equality are both seen as threats to the model of male dominance and by extension are seen as threats to the church and the nation. Arguing that the central purpose of marriage is procreation serves the interests of those who believe in the value of a patriarchal family structure, because it assigns women a limited and subordinate role and it bars gay and lesbian people from marriage.[22]

Jerry Falwell, in his bestselling book, *Listen America!* warned that changes in gender roles and the acceptance of gay and lesbian people were two sides of the same coin. Falwell proclaimed, "We would not be having the present moral crisis regarding the homosexual movement if men and women accepted their proper roles as designated by God. . . . In the Christian home the father is responsible to exercise spiritual control and to be the head over his wife and children. . . . In the Christian home, the woman is to be submissive. . . . Homosexuality is Satan's diabolical attack upon the family, God's order in Creation."[23]

In 2003, Glenn Stanton, director of social research and cultural affairs at Focus on the Family, warned that if gay and lesbian people were allowed to marry, "the terms 'husband' and 'wife' would become merely words with no meaning. Gender would become nothing."[24] It is essential to the conservative "defense of marriage" that husbands have a superior role to wives. If two people of the same sex were allowed to marry, it would ratify the transformation of marriage that has been going on over the past thirty years, as people have developed more egalitarian ideas of their roles in marriage relationships.

James Dobson, founder of Focus on the Family (and its political arm, Focus on the Family Action), is perhaps the most vocal advocate of the strict-father model of male dominance as the ideal for the family, the church, and the nation.[25] *U.S. News & World Report* called Dobson "the best-known leader among America's 50 million-strong evangelical Christians."[26] The two most important political issues for Dobson and his followers are opposition to abortion and opposition to marriage of gay and lesbian people (notice how these two priorities serve to reinforce traditional gender roles). "You have to decide the things that matter most," he declares, ". . . if that makes us sound extreme, I'll take it."[27]

Dobson has announced, "We're involved in what is known as a culture war that is aimed right straight at the institution of the family."[28] Who is responsible for this attack on the family? Listen to statements from Dobson's Focus on the Family: "For more than 40 years, the homosexual activist movement has sought to implement a master plan that has had as its centerpiece the utter destruction of the family."[29] "They don't just want marriage. They want to destroy marriage and the family as we know it."[30] "Traditional marriage between one man and one woman cannot co-exist with homosexual marriage. It will destroy the family."[31] If you look closely at Dobson's statements, his real aim is to fight against any change in gender roles in society. Same-sex marriage, feminism, and any sort of evolution in the perceived purpose of marriage are all seen as threats to traditional heterosexual male dominance of family and society.

A striking illustration of how important male gender superiority is to Dobson came in 1997 when Dobson ran advertisements in Christian magazines questioning the trustworthiness of a proposed "gender-inclusive" translation of the popular New International Version (NIV) of the New Testament; the proposed translation would have substituted gender-neutral words, such as "people," for gender-specific words, such as "mankind." In a March 29, 1997, cover story, conservative *World* magazine's Susan Olasky had reported that NIV translators were conspiring to produce an edition of the Bible that would represent a "feminist seduction" of the evangelical church by changing pronouns and gender references.[32] In *World*, Dobson attacked the members of the NIV translation committee: "The Committee on Bible Translation (CBT) and executives of Zondervan Publishing House are editing the inspired words of God himself . . . degenderizing the biblical text and inserting words that are not represented in the source documents."[33] He proclaimed, "Frankly, I find it breath-taking that the CBT or any other group would feel justified in editing the utterances of the Holy One of Israel."

Dobson invited eleven men—four involved in translating or publishing the NIV, and seven critics of inclusive language—to a meeting about the translation. They included leaders of the Council on Biblical Manhood and Womanhood, a group that proclaims male headship, plus representatives of denominations opposed to the ordination of women. The group produced thirteen "Guidelines for Translation of Gender-Related Language in Scripture," which among other things demanded that the term "man" be used as a designation for the human race or human beings.[34] As a result of the criticism, the International Bible Society and Zondervan Publishing Company announced that they would scrap the proposed NIV translation.[35]

Many conservative Christian scholars looked askance at the "translation guidelines" developed by the ad hoc group that Dobson had convened. They deplored the confusion of issues regarding the accuracy of translation with attempts to maintain a traditional cultural position of male dominance.[36] A woman New Testament scholar at Gordon-Conwell Theological Seminary, Aída Besançon Spencer, wrote, "Indeed, the guidelines represent an attempt by one gender, men, to hold on to power even when that means thwarting the accuracy of the biblical text and the good news it proclaims."[37] An editorial in the magazine *Christianity Today* asked if evangelicals were entering a new phase of "fundamentalist political correctness."[38]

When the views of Dobson's ad hoc committee on translation guidelines were criticized by other conservative Christian scholars as "linguistically and hermeneutically naïve and inaccurate," Dobson admitted, "I am not a biblical scholar [and] I don't have the academic qualifications to debate [these issues]."[39] He nonetheless continued to assert his cultural biases, as if they were biblically accurate, in the name of preserving his vision of the ideal American family.

It is important to note that in his work Dobson isn't defending families, marriage, or the Bible. He is defending male privilege and power. Dobson has said, "God designed man to be the aggressor, provider, and leader in his family. Somehow that is tied to his sex drive."[40]

Dobson's approach denies the full expression of gifts that God has bestowed on both women and men. As a church, when we include the views and experiences of people of color, women, persons with disabilities, the young, the elderly, and people who are homosexual, we are all wonderfully enriched.

Opposition to Science

Despite having a PhD from the University of Southern California in child development, Dobson rejects reputable scientific studies and the judgments of professional scientific associations in order to defend his view of the male-dominant model of marriage, family, and society.[41] His positions are regularly contradicted by professional scientific and medical associations. For example, Dobson and the few conservative Christian organizations that he relies on[42] insist that homosexuality is a mental disorder.[43] However, in 1973 the American Psychiatric Association voted to no longer consider homosexuality a mental disorder, and the American Psychological Association took a similar action in 1975.[44]

Nor is homosexuality considered a psychiatric disorder. For a mental condition to be described as a psychiatric disorder, it should either regularly cause emotional distress or regularly be associated with clinically significant impairment of social functioning.[45] In 1994, the American Psychiatric Association and the American Psychological Association stated: "The research on homosexuality is very clear. Homosexuality is neither mental illness nor moral depravity. It is simply the way a minority of our population expresses human love and sexuality. Study after study documents the mental health of gay men and lesbians. Studies of judgment, stability, reliability, and social and vocational adaptiveness all show that gay men and lesbians function every bit as well as heterosexuals."[46]

Dobson and his colleagues make the charge that "homosexuality is a gender identity disorder."[47] "Homosexuality is a masculine inferiority"—the result of having an overemotionally involved mother and a withdrawn, nonexpressive father.[48] Dobson's assertion is simply not true. In 1981, researchers from the Kinsey Institute published the results of a comprehensive study on sexual preference among women and men. They conducted lengthy interviews with nearly 1,000 homosexual people and 500 heterosexual people. "The investigators assessed nearly every imaginable psychological cause of homosexuality—parental relationships, childhood sexual experiences, peer relationships, dating experiences. Their findings: Apart from homosexuals' somewhat greater nonconformity, the reported backgrounds of homosexuals and heterosexuals were similar. Homosexuals were no more likely to have been smothered by maternal love, neglected by their father, or sexually abused."[49] The American Psychoanalytic Association, in its position statement on the treatment of homosexual patients (1997), indicates that Dobson's attitudes may create problems rather than curing them: "Same-gender sexual orientation cannot be assumed to represent a deficit in personality development or the expression of psychopathology. As with any societal prejudice, anti-homosexual bias negatively affects mental health, contributing to an enduring sense of stigma and pervasive self-criticism in people of same-gender sexual orientation through the internalization of such prejudice."[50]

Dobson's views on homosexuality in relation to marriage and family life are refuted by recent statements of the American Anthropological Association, the world's largest organization of people who study culture. In its 2004 "Statement on Marriage and the Family" the association declared,

> The results of more than a century of anthropological research on households, kinship relationships, and families, across cultures and through time, provide no support whatsoever for the view that either civilization or viable social orders depend upon marriage as an exclusively heterosexual institution. Rather, anthropological research supports the conclusion that a vast array of family types, including families built upon same-sex partnerships, can contribute to stable and humane societies. The Executive Board of the American Anthropological Association strongly opposes a constitutional amendment limiting marriage to heterosexual couples.[51]

The American Association for Marriage and Family Therapy annual conference in September 2004 stated, "We see no evidence that same-sex couples or family units vary significantly from heterosexual couples or family units in terms of aspirations, hopes and goals, or in outcomes for children."[52]

Joseph Nicolosi, president of the National Association for Research and Therapy of Homosexuality, a frequent speaker at Dobson-sponsored conferences, articulated the Freudian position that homosexuality is caused by poor parenting and could be prevented or cured.[53] Nicolosi said: "We advise parents to use clear and consistent messages: 'We do not accept your effeminacy. You are a boy. God made you a boy. Being a boy is special.' When parents do this, especially fathers, they can turn their boys around."[54] "Focus on the Family is promoting the truth that homosexuality is preventable and treatable . . . individuals don't have to be gay."[55]

Countering this position, the American Academy of Pediatrics states: "Therapy directed specifically at changing sexual orientation is contraindicated, since it can provoke guilt and anxiety while having little or no potential for achieving changes in orientation."[56] Also opposing the stance of Focus on the Family, and critical of the assumption that people who are homosexual should and can change their sexual orientation, are the American Psychiatric Association, the American Medical Association, the American Psychological Association, the American Counseling Association, and the National Association of Social Workers.[57] Together these organizations represent more than 477,000 health and mental health professionals. Collectively they have come to the conclusion that "homosexuality is not a mental disorder and thus there is no need for a 'cure.'"[58]

Dobson and his colleagues paint the very worst picture of people who are homosexual. They compare people who are homosexual to prostitutes, pedophiles, adulterers, and people who prefer animals sexually.[59] They claim that it is not possible for a homosexual to be a totally healthy person.[60] They assert that promiscuity is the defining feature of male homosexuality.[61] None of these claims can be demonstrated by objective research. Real Christian gay and lesbian people living in faithful, committed relationships bear no resemblances to Dobson's caricatures.

In a statement reminiscent of Charles Hodge's opposition to evolution in the nineteenth century, James Dobson has said, "Science can be a wonderful instrument of good as long as it respects the bound of moral principles."[62] Hodge claimed that science was to be ignored when it departed from the Scottish Common Sense philosophy that he espoused. Similarly, Dobson rejects all scientific studies that do not conform to the fundamentalist worldview that he espouses.[63]

Violent Rhetoric

The opposition to homosexuality by religious fundamentalists is not just a matter of differing ideas. The tone of fundamentalist opposition is often crude and violent. Focus on the Family says, "The homosexual agenda is a beast. [It] wants our kids. . . . And the only thing that's standing between them and that agenda . . . are those of us who believe in the Judeo-Christian values of this country."[64]

In 2004 televangelist Jimmy Swaggart announced to his audience, "I've never seen a man in my life I wanted to marry. . . . And I'm gonna be blunt and plain, if one ever looks at me like that, I'm going to kill him and tell God he died. . . . In case anybody doesn't know, God calls it an abomination."[65]

Amazingly, in the midst of such violent rhetoric and ongoing physical violence against gays and lesbians, such as the murder of Matthew Shepherd, conservative advocacy groups such as the National Religious Broadcasters association (an umbrella group of some 1,600 Christian radio and TV broadcasters) and the politically influential Family Research Council have actually mobilized to *oppose* passage of any hate-crime legislation that includes protections for gay and lesbian people.[66]

In response to such violent attitudes, Coretta Scott King has said, "Homophobia is like racism and anti-Semitism and other forms of bigotry in that it seeks to dehumanize a large group of people, to deny their humanity, their dignity and personhood."[67]

I find great wisdom in the reasoned view of the late evangelical ethicist Lewis B. Smedes, who asked: "What danger to straight people is posed by homosexuals? Some say that they are a threat to the family, but none tell us how. Some fear that they might abuse our children, but no facts have ever been adduced to show that they are any more likely to do so than heterosexual people are. Do homosexuals threaten to invade our homes, steal our property, rape our daughters? What we know is that homosexual men are murdered by heterosexual people just for being gay; what we also know is that there is no record of a heterosexual being murdered for not being gay. Why, then, I wonder, in a world of violence, starving children, cruel tyrannies, and natural disasters, are Christian people so steamed up about the harmless and often beneficent presence of gays and lesbians among us?"[68]

The Irony in the Debate over Marriage

Newsweek in spring 2004 was honest about the current state of marriage in America: "If marriage is in trouble, don't blame gays. Straights changed the rules."[69] Let us take a realistic look, for a moment, at the state of marriage in the United States. In the last one hundred years, the United States has gone from being the most marrying society in the world to the one with the most divorces and single-parent families.[70] Among all the industrialized nations, the United States has the highest rate of teenage pregnancy and teenage childbirth, despite having the highest rate of teenage abortions.[71] An estimated one-third of American children live without their biological father present.[72]

In the U.S.A., "8.1% of coupled households are made up of unmarried, heterosexual partners."[73] A Barna poll in 2001 found that cohabitation—living with a member of the opposite sex without marriage—has been practiced at some time by 33 percent of all adults and 25 percent of born-again Christians.[74] While some view living together as a sort of trial marriage, 40 percent of those cohabiting do not marry.[75] We live in an era of family disruption that leads sociologists to talk of an "emerging culture of 'serial marriage' and 'nonmarriage.'"[76]

None of these alarming trends has been caused by homosexuals who want to marry.[77] None will be solved by denying same-sex couples the right to marry. In a culture of "nonmarriage" it is ironic that we are spending great amounts of money and energy in trying to prevent people from marrying who want to do so in a way that would contribute to the stability of society.

The legal rights conferred by marriage are vast. U.S. Representative Henry J. Hyde, as chairperson of the House Committee on the Judiciary, asked the General Accounting Office (GAO) "to identify federal laws in which benefits, rights and privileges are contingent on marital status." The response of the GAO, in a letter of January 31, 1997, ran to seventy-five pages. Married heterosexual couples living in the U.S.A. are entitled to 1,049 federal rights, benefits, and privileges. Depending on the state in which a couple lives, there may be as many as 400 additional legal benefits. Most of these legal and economic benefits cannot be privately contracted for or arranged. Lesbian and gay couples, especially those with children, understandably wish to be able to provide in these myriad ways for their families.[78]

Perhaps the greatest irony in the marriage debate is that self-described born-again Christians, a segment of the population that is often vocal about supporting bans on same-sex marriage, seem to exhibit greater problems with their own marriages. Evangelical pollster George Barna found that during the 1990s born-again Christians had higher divorce rates than non-Christians.[79] Professor Brad Wilcox, a Christian sociologist who specializes in family issues, notes that "compared with the rest of the population, conservative Protestants are *more* likely to divorce." He also points out that divorce rates are higher in the southern United States, where conservative Protestants make up a higher percentage of the population.[80] The states of Kentucky, Mississippi, and Arkansas, which voted overwhelmingly for constitutional amendments to ban same-sex marriage in 2004, had three of the highest divorce rates in the United States. In contrast, the state with the lowest divorce rate is Massachusetts, a state whose Supreme Court has ruled in favor of gay marriage.[81] There is clearly a disconnect between the problems facing heterosexual marriages in the United States and the conservatives' proposed solution of banning same-sex marriage.

The allegation that allowing gay and lesbian people to marry will destroy heterosexual marriage is nonsense! It is simply a diversion from dealing with the real problems of heterosexual marriage. We have heard this kind of inflated rhetoric before from respected church people. If blacks were allowed to vote, it would be the end of "civilization itself" (Robert Lewis Dabney, 1867).[82] If women were not kept subordinate to men, we would soon have a country "from which all order and all virtue would speedily be banished" (Charles Hodge, 1838).[83] These men were the leading theologians of their day. They were quite sincere in their concern. They were also dead wrong.

The current effort to prevent people who are gay or lesbian from getting married is a diversion that makes Christian people feel they are doing something to defend marriage, but it does absolutely nothing to address the real problems of marriage in the United States.

Real Marriage for Real People

On February 28, 2004, I received an award from the Lazarus Project, a ministry of reconciliation between gay and straight people in southern

California. As I was preparing my speech for the awards dinner, the national battle lines in the fight over same-sex marriage shifted dramatically. On February 10, San Francisco mayor Gavin Newsom ordered the County Clerk to end discrimination against same-sex couples in issuing marriage licenses. Two days later, the county began to issue marriage licenses to same-sex couples. Over the next several weeks, more than 4,000 gay and lesbian couples were married.[84]

Two impressions struck me as I looked at the newspaper pictures of people waiting for marriage licenses in San Francisco. The first was how happy they looked. This was not a political protest; it was evidence of love and the joy that marriage brings. The second was how many had children with them. These were people who loved and cared for children and wanted the respect and benefits that come with marriage for the good of their children.[85]

The events of that period in San Francisco gave the lie to stereotypes of gay and lesbian people. These were people who are just like those of us who are heterosexual and who want to live stable, faithful lives to which they were willing to be publicly committed. There was nothing broken about them; they did not need to be fixed. We just need to quit slamming the door in their face.

Yet that is what the president of the United States is trying to do. As same-sex marriages were being performed in San Francisco, George W. Bush announced, "If we are to prevent the meaning of marriage from being changed forever, our nation must enact a constitutional amendment to protect marriage in America."[86] In 217 years of American history, there have only been seventeen amendments to the Constitution. They fall into two categories: to expand civil rights and to fix problems in the structure of government. The only one that didn't fit in one of these two categories was prohibition of "intoxicating liquors," and we all know how that one turned out![87] "No amendment has ever chiseled exclusion and discrimination *into* the U.S. Constitution. Yet that is what an amendment banning gay marriage proposes to do."[88]

My Experience of Gay and Lesbian Couples

It seems to me that all human beings, gay and straight, deserve the opportunity to have the companionship of another person with whom they have formed a covenant of lifelong, loving commitment. When I was Moderator of the General Assembly in 2001–2002, my wife,

Sharon, and I were invited to the lovely home of Doug and Dennis for dinner and an evening of conversation with gay and lesbian couples and their friends. We met two elderly gentlemen, Dick and Jim, who at that time had been together for forty-seven years. One of them told me that he lived every day of his life in fear that they would be "outed" and that he would lose his job. Yet they persisted in caring for one another. Many of the couples there had been together twenty years or more, and all of them ten years or more.[89] I remember a heterosexual friend telling me that in her circle of friends anyone who had stayed married for more than five years was an exceptional case. The people I met at Doug and Dennis's house were just ordinary, faithful Christians who displayed a profound commitment to each other.

I know many lesbian couples and gay couples who manifest remarkable faithfulness in their commitment to a single partner, despite all of the roadblocks that society and the church put in their way. Just a few days before I wrote this, I spoke with a lesbian couple, Cheryl and Debbie, after church. One was carrying an eight-week-old baby in her arms, and the other was carrying the child's car seat. They looked like every set of new parents—radiant and happy. Despite conservative claims to the contrary, studies show no discernable difference in good adjustment between children raised by a male-female couple and those raised by a same-sex couple.[90] Indeed, a few weeks after Cheryl and Debbie adopted their daughter, the agency called and asked if they would take a little boy—and they did.

I also know a gay couple, Tim and Dan, who have adopted two special-needs children—children often least desired by adoptive couples. They were foster parents for many years, caring for many special-needs children and hoping each time that they would be allowed to adopt them. Finally they were given permission and have even changed jobs and relocated to a community where they felt their children would be accepted and could get the best education.

I had the privilege of being with a gay couple, Neil and John, who had just been married in San Francisco during that brief window of opportunity opened by Mayor Newsom. Their story of several attempts to be at the right place and right time to get a license was hilarious and deeply touching. They love each other and wanted to make public and celebrate their commitment to each other.

I know several friends who tried not to be homosexual, who entered into heterosexual relationships, married, and had children. Then, at some point, they could no longer deny who they really were and went through the painful process of separation and divorce. Finding someone whom they could love and support has freed them to be the person God intended for them to be. How much pain could have been avoided if these people had been allowed, in the beginning, to marry someone with whom they were really compatible!

I also think of several former missionaries that I know who are gay. One broke his engagement on his wedding day and remained single. Another has remained faithfully married to his wife for a lifetime while acknowledging that he is a gay man. Yet another was married to a woman briefly and then lived for years feeling that he could never know love. Originally a Presbyterian, he came to know the founder of the Metropolitan Community Church, Troy Perry, a former pastor in the Church of God,[91] and helped Perry develop a curriculum for the denomination's Bible School. In that process he met and fell in love with a man who loved him; and they have been together for over twenty years, as responsible members of their community. These gay men made different choices and have different histories. But this is the same: they are faithful Christians whose primary desire is to serve God and live responsibly as the people God created them to be.

A while back I attended a public discussion where four different aspects of the issue of homosexuality were being discussed, each with a pro and a con speaker. Hal Schell, a Presbyterian who often represented the position that gays could change their behavior to heterosexuality, spoke against accepting "unrepentant" homosexuals into church leadership. He presented the case, which some conservatives would like to claim as normative, that childhood abuse (physical and sexual) had caused him to live a life of promiscuous gay sex. A former Fuller Seminary colleague, Mel White, was the other speaker on the topic of experience. Mel genuinely empathized with Hal's experience: "No one should be treated like that."

However, Mel's life experience was just the opposite. He had a loving family, was successful at everything he attempted in school. The only difference was that, as Mel put it, at football games while the other guys were looking at the cheerleaders, he was attracted to the quarterback. Mel's autobiography, *Stranger at the Gate,* is the poignant story of a deeply religious, theologically conservative, highly successful minister, writer, and filmmaker who struggled all his life with the reality that he was gay and finally admitted it to himself and his family.[92] He now heads Soulforce, a movement modeled on the nonviolent resistance of Gandhi and Martin Luther King Jr., whose purpose is to stop the spiritual violence against God's lesbian, gay, bisexual, and transgender children by telling the truth about them to the churches.[93]

I am not claiming that people who are homosexual are perfect. In my experience, they are just human beings with the normal hopes and fears, struggles and challenges of others in the population. However, given the ugly and baseless allegations that are made about people who are homosexual as a class, it is important to point out that these stereotypes are just not true.

A Wideness in God's Mercy

During my year as Moderator, Sharon and I also had the privilege of visiting the Netherlands, where we had lived for five years during the 1960s while I worked on my doctorate and Sharon taught school. I was a graduate student at the Free University, related to the Reformed churches in the Netherlands, and I was the organizing pastor of an English-speaking congregation that was related to the older Netherlands Reformed Church. At the time, these two Dutch Calvinist denominations did not get along, but now, by God's grace, they have merged with the small Evangelical Lutheran Church, to form the Protestant Church in the Netherlands. I had the privilege of addressing the Trio-Synode, the gathering of all three denominations as they prepared for merger.

All three of these denominations already ordain gay and lesbian people to church office. Sexual orientation is just not an issue for them. In the Netherlands, where the Reformed tradition is woven into the fabric of society, gay and lesbian people can also be married.[94]

The late Lewis Smedes, my former colleague at Fuller Seminary, did his doctorate at the Free University in Amsterdam ten years before me. We had both imbibed deeply of Dutch Calvinism. In 1999 Lew, recalling a line from an old hymn, "There's a wideness in God's mercy like the wideness of the sea," argued that the church should accept people who are homosexual as full members. His last line was, "I think I know my own heart well enough to believe that if [God's] mercy is wide enough for me, it is wide enough for them."[95]

The Lazarus Project takes its name from Jesus' call to the dead Lazarus to "come out" of his tomb. Those who have "come out" as gay and lesbian people are simply asking the church to let all Christians come in. When we realize how gracious God has been to us, we cannot deny God's grace to others.

The church should be first, and not last in offering this welcome. The Bible tells us so. In the book of Revelation, the Risen Christ is represented as saying: "Look, I have set before you an open door, which no one is able to shut" (Rev. 3:8). Jesus has opened a door through which every one of us can enter into God's realm.

There are gay and lesbian people in most of our churches. When they can be full and equal members we will all be blessed. The possibility that we can fully include all of our members in the life of the church is within reach. It requires only that we be true to the fundamental teachings of the Christian faith. In chapter 7, I suggest how we can do this in the Presbyterian Church and how it will resolve our present conflict.

7

Recommendations for the Presbyterian Church (U.S.A.)

It seems to me that the church and every person within the church is faced with a choice: to witness to an ancient Near Eastern cultural bias of male gender superiority, or to witness to Jesus Christ and his redemptive life and ministry. The best methods of biblical interpretation, from the Reformation on down through today, urge us to reject narrow historical and cultural bias and instead to follow Jesus' example. The purpose of the Bible is not to forever weld us to an ancient culture. The purpose of the Bible is to tell us the story of Jesus' life, death, and resurrection.

Those who choose to witness to ancient cultural bias will always be able to find certain passages, take them out of context, and turn them into church laws that benefit them and discriminate against those whom they dislike. Those who choose to follow Jesus will see Jesus as the center of the biblical story and interpret each passage in light of his ministry. Using this Christ-centered approach enriches our understanding of the gospel and brings us into a closer relationship with God and our fellow human beings.

HEALING THE CHURCH

If you believe, as I do, that homosexuality is not a sin and is not prohibited by the Bible, then the next question becomes, how do we heal the church of this injustice that has divided us? Clearly, policies, by-laws and church constitutions in some cases, will need to be amended.

But it seems to me that the first step is for all of us in the church to apologize, institutionally, collectively, and personally. By condemning people who are gay and lesbian and barring them from marriage and holding office in the church, we have caused an enormous amount of unnecessary suffering, while distorting Jesus' message of love. If we reach out to our lesbian, gay, bisexual, and transgender sisters and brothers and show that we truly understand that we have caused them pain, it will speed the healing process—for everyone.

There are precedents for denominational apologies. In 1995, for example, on the occasion of its 150th anniversary, the Southern Baptist Convention (SBC) officially apologized for "condoning" racism. The SBC resolution in part stated, "We apologize to all African Americans for condoning and/or perpetuating individual and systemic racism in our lifetime, and we genuinely repent of racism of which we have been guilty, whether consciously or unconsciously." Gary Frost, a black pastor who is an SBC second vice president, formally accepted the apology. He said, "We pray that the genuineness of your repentance will be reflected in your attitudes and in your actions."[1]

In 2001, Presbyterians asked the forgiveness of African Americans for slavery and segregation. The 213th General Assembly said, "We acknowledge, however, our church's common complicity in the institution of slavery and its oppressive inequities that linger to this day."[2] Two hundred thirteen years is a long time to wait for an apology. Think of how much good it would have done for our church and our nation to apologize immediately after emancipation—to immediately begin the hard emotional task of healing our churches and communities.

How long will we wait before we apologize for the sin of homophobia, "the irrational fear of and contempt for homosexual persons"?[3] If we believe the church has committed an injustice, we can drag our feet and engage in begrudging half measures for decades. Or we can turn and face our mistakes, deal constructively with them now, and move forward together again as one church family. What often makes official apologies, like the recent Southern Baptist and the Presbyterian apologies, seem hollow, is that they are offered by people who themselves did not commit the original offense, to people who did not suffer from the original discrimination. How much more appropriate and effective would be an apology offered now to people who are homosexual, by people who, even passively and unintentionally, have been participant in their oppression.

An apology, personally and collectively, would be a good first step. But progress requires more than words. We need to demonstrate the depth of our understanding of Christ's message through action. We need to give LGBT people full and equal rights within the church and work for their rights within the broader society. That means marriage, ordination, and every other right necessary to bring people who are homosexual into full equality with people who are heterosexual. As full and equal human beings they deserve full participation under church and civil law. It is that simple. No three-fifths compromise. No separate but equal.

The trajectory of Christian history is in the direction of ever-greater openness and inclusiveness. We rejoice now in the leadership in our churches of people of color, women, and divorced and remarried people. The time will come when having gay, lesbian, bisexual, and transgender people in Christian leadership will be just as routine.

Each denomination can work out its own repentance in the way that is most appropriate and effective for it. In what follows, I point to the barriers that my denomination, the Presbyterian Church (U.S.A.), must remove so that all of our members can have the full rights of membership.

SOURCES OF AUTHORITY AND GUIDANCE

In all Christian denominations, the Bible is the primary source of authority and guidance. Most denominations also have subordinate standards, that is, statements of faith, written at particular times and places to expound and interpret the meaning of Scripture for a particular people. These officially adopted documents articulate a church's "understanding of the meaning and implications of the one basic confession of the lordship of Christ."[4] These statements of faith are in various settings called creeds, confessions, symbols, formulas, definitions, declarations of faith, statements of belief, and articles of faith.[5] Roman Catholics, Eastern Orthodox, Lutherans, and Presbyterians have statements adopted by ecclesiastical bodies as official expressions of their faith. Some churches, such as Anglican, Episcopal, and Methodist, have documents to which they look for guidance that have a slightly lower official status. Even so-called "free" churches, like Baptists, which claim they follow only the Bible, often have semiauthoritative statements that can be very influential in guiding beliefs and behaviors.[6]

These subordinate standards can be very helpful in providing clarifying summaries of the main teachings of Scripture. They can also, however, create problems when they take particular teachings out of context and make them church law. In most cases, it is the policies and procedures in these subordinate standards that will need to be amended in order to grant equal rights in the church to people who are homosexual.

The Presbyterian Constitution

Presbyterians have two subordinate standards that together form their *Constitution*: the *Book of Confessions* and the *Book of Order*. The *Book of Confessions* contains eleven theological documents. Two are ancient creeds: the Nicene Creed and the Apostles' Creed. Three date from the sixteenth-century Reformation: the Scots Confession of 1560; the Heidelberg Catechism of 1563; and the Second Helvetic Confession, published in 1566. Three come from the seventeenth-century Puritan Reformation in England: the Westminster Confession of Faith; the Shorter Catechism; and the Larger Catechism. The final three are twentieth-century documents: the Theological Declaration of Barmen (1934); the Confession of 1967; and A Brief Statement of Faith—Presbyterian Church (U.S.A.), adopted in 1991.

The *Book of Order* spells out the way in which the Christian faith, expressed in Scripture and summarized in the *Book of Confessions,* is to be applied in the ongoing life of the Presbyterian Church. It consists of three parts: the Form of Government; the Directory for Worship; and the Rules of Discipline.

American Presbyterians prize their *Constitution*, which, in rudimentary form, came into being at approximately the same time as the United States Constitution. Since the Presbyterian *Constitution* functions to interpret and apply Scripture, any flaws in it assume critical importance. At the same time, we acknowledge that human beings who create the *Constitution* can make mistakes. The Westminster Confession of Faith acknowledges the fragile character of human decisions: "All synods or councils since the apostles' times, whether general or particular, may err, and many have erred; therefore they are not to be made the rule of faith or practice, but to be used as a help in both."[7]

Unfortunately, American Presbyterians recently have erred in using and amending their *Constitution* in ways that violate its essential values. As I discuss below, we have *unintentionally* accepted a flaw in the *Book of Confessions* by adopting a recent translation of the Heidelberg Catechism that adds a phrase that condemns people who are homosexual—

a phrase that is not in the original document. What is worse, the church has *intentionally* incorporated a flaw in the *Book of Order* by voting to amend it to take away from people who are homosexual the right to hold ordained office in the church.[8]

These two flawed statements in the Presbyterian *Constitution* distort its general principles. Our history demonstrates that when an exception is made to fundamental principles, it turns out to be a mistake that must later be rescinded. The flaws in both the *Book of Confessions* and the *Book of Order* need to be removed in order for the church to uphold its best principles and practices.

Principles in the *Book of Confessions*

In its confessional statements, the church declares to its members and the world "who and what it is, what it believes, what it resolves to do."[9] The confessions "summarize the essence of Christian tradition."[10]

Although changing anything in the *Book of Confessions* requires a more exacting process than changing rules for government, worship, or discipline in the *Book of Order*, the confessions *can* be changed. The church is "reformed," rooted in the biblical and ecclesiastical tradition, and "always reforming," or being reformed, changed, "according to the Word of God and the call of the Spirit."

The content of the *Book of Confessions* is summarized in chapter 2 of the *Book of Order*, so we have an idea of the broad and enduring themes Presbyterians share with other Christians. First, we share with the universal Christian church "the mystery of the triune God and of the incarnation of the eternal Word of God in Jesus Christ."[11] Second, we are thankful inheritors of the Protestant Reformation with its watchwords of "grace alone, faith alone, Scripture alone."[12] Third, we acknowledge some emphases of the particular Reformed family to which we belong: God's sovereignty; election of people for salvation and service; covenant life marked by order according to the Word of God; stewardship of God's creation; recognition of the sin of idolatry; seeking justice and living in obedience to the Word of God.[13] None of these doctrines is the exclusive property of Presbyterians. Note that in chapter 2 of the *Book of Order* they are stated as broad themes of Christian consensus, not as the particular opinions of one party in the church.

The confessions, like the Bible, should be interpreted by taking into account their linguistic, historical, and cultural contexts. That means that we are not bound by particular ideas in the confessions that reflect the prejudices and limitations of a given culture or time.[14] A few examples will clarify what I mean:

1. The Westminster Larger Catechism evidences an ethic that supports a rigid class system in which there are "superiors" and "inferiors."[15] In contrast, A Brief Statement of Faith, adopted in 1991, recognizes that God "makes everyone equally in God's image, male and female, of every race and people, to live as one community."[16]

2. In 1930s Germany, the German Christian Movement accepted the Nazi party's demand that Jews, homosexuals, and the disabled be excluded from the church and society. In response, the Confessing Church rose up and in 1934 developed the Barmen Declaration, which declares as its first principle that "Jesus Christ, as he is attested for us in Holy Scripture, is the one Word of God which we have to hear and which we have to trust and obey in life and in death."[17] Therefore it concludes, "The church's commission, upon which its freedom is founded, consists in delivering the message of the free grace of God to *all* people in Christ's stead."[18]

3. The Confession of 1967, modeled on the Barmen Declaration, calls for reconciliation and the abolition of racial segregation. It states as a fundamental principle, "Congregations, individuals, or groups of Christians who exclude, dominate, or patronize their fellowmen [*sic*], however subtly, resist the Spirit of God and bring contempt on the faith which they profess."[19]

As we can see, the trajectory of the confessions, like the trajectory of the church, is clearly in the direction of acceptance and inclusion of all people, based on the love of God in Jesus Christ. Therefore, to use an inauthentic statement in the *Book of Confessions* to exclude thousands of people, despite their faithful commitment to Jesus Christ, is to misrepresent the content and misunderstand the function of this invaluable part of our Presbyterian *Constitution*.

A Flaw in the *Book of Confessions*

As I explained in chapter 4, the Reformed confessions, properly understood, do not condemn homosexuality. In fact, the Reformed confessions say very little about sexuality itself. Yet most Presbyterians mistakenly believe that the confessions contain a clear prohibition against homosexuality. So where does that mistaken belief come from?

In January 2001, I was preparing to teach a class on the Reformed confessions at San Francisco Theological Seminary's Southern California campus. One of my favorite confessional texts is the Heidelberg Catechism. It was written and published in 1563 to ensure a Reformed, rather than Lutheran, understanding of the Christian faith in the palatinate (like a small state) of Heidelberg, in what is now Germany. The elector, or governor, Frederick III, had entrusted the writing of the catechism to two young men: Zacharius Ursinus, who at twenty-seven was the head of the College of Wisdom, the local theological seminary; and Caspar Olevianus, who at age twenty-six was the senior pastor of the Holy Ghost Church, the cathedral church in Heidelberg.

In my teaching I try to relate the doctrines of the confessions to current issues in our denomination. The Presbyterian Church had been struggling with the issue of the ordination of people who are gay or lesbian since 1976, and we appeared ready to do pitched battle over this issue again at the 2001 General Assembly. With that in mind, I was especially interested in Question and Answer 87 in the Heidelberg Catechism [emphasis added]:

Q. 87. Can those who do not turn to God from their ungrateful, impenitent life be saved?

A. Certainly not! Scripture says, "Surely you know that the unjust will never come into possession of the kingdom of God. Make no mistake: no fornicator or idolater, none who are guilty either of adultery or of *homosexual perversion*, no thieves or grabbers or drunkards or slanderers or swindlers, will possess the kingdom of God."[20]

That seemed to be clear evidence in favor of the denomination's current policy of calling all homosexual behavior sinful and, on that basis, of barring gay and lesbian people from office in the church.

That would have been the end of the discussion, except for my memory that when people began using the *Book of Confessions* in arguments against homosexuality, Johanna Bos, a professor at Louisville Presbyterian Theological Seminary, had noted that the text of Answer 87 of the Heidelberg Catechism was not authentic.[21] In fact, a footnote in the *Book of Confessions* indicates that this translation of the Heidelberg Catechism had its origin in the early 1960s, when the Reformed Church in America and the World Alliance of Reformed Churches produced a 400th anniversary edition of the Heidelberg Catechism, originally written in 1563.[22] The text of the Heidelberg Catechism in our *Book of Confessions* was taken from that 400th-anniversary translation.

Johanna Bos noticed a difference between earlier translations and the 1962 edition because she was born and raised in the Netherlands. There, as a youth, she received rigorous training in the Heidelberg Catechism, along with the Belgic Confession and the Canons of Dort, which together comprise the three doctrinal statements of the Dutch Reformed churches. It was common practice in the Reformed churches of the Netherlands for pastors to spend several years taking young people carefully through the catechism in preparation for their joining the church, usually at about age eighteen. Furthermore, Dutch Reformed pastors were obliged to preach through the catechism each year at the evening service. Bos said that, despite all of her study in the Netherlands, she had never heard any mention of homosexuality. My interest and curiosity were aroused.

At the Huntington Library in San Marino, California, I discovered a significant number of editions of the Heidelberg Catechism, available only in the rare book room. I read Question and Answer 87 in the original Latin version of Zacharius Ursinus, in a work published in 1586.[23] I followed that with a German version from 1795.[24] (Olevianus is believed to have translated Ursinus's Latin version into German.) Then I went to more familiar territory and read a Dutch version of the catechism, published along with a Psalm book, from 1591.[25] I found and consulted a 1645 English edition published in London during the meeting of the Westminster Assembly,[26] and I concluded my catechism inquiry by studying a 1765 English translation of the catechism prepared for the Dutch Reformed Church in New York.[27]

Answer 87 was the same in the Latin original and all of these early translations. The list of those impenitent sinners excluded from the kingdom of God was always, in the same order, "unchaste person, idolater, adulterer, thief, covetous man, drunkard, slanderer, robber, or any such like." In *none* of the texts was there even a word where the 1962 version of the Heidelberg inserted the phrase, "homosexual perversion." In every case, the list went from adulterer to thief, with no intervening word or phrase that could have been rendered "homosexual perversion."

The early editions of the catechism provide Scripture references in the margin. For Question and Answer 87 the texts are always 1 Corinthians 6:9–10; Ephesians 5:5; 1 John 3:14–15; and Galatians 5:21. At this point, I remembered that some years ago I had heard that the phrase "homosexual perversion" in the 1962 version of Answer

87 in the Heidelberg Catechism was taken from the translation of 1 Corinthians 6:9–10 in the New English Bible.[28]

Puzzled, I contacted the chair of a committee in the Reformed Church of America that had produced a more current version of the Heidelberg Catechism in 1989. One member of that translation team had also been one of the two translators of the 1962 version of the catechism. I contacted that person, and he acknowledged that the translators of the 1962 version had inserted into the catechism the wording of 1 Corinthians 6:9–10 as it appears in the New English Bible, which had been published in 1961 and was at the time the newest available translation. The phrase "homosexual perversion" was used for the first time in that 1961 NEB translation.

The words in Greek that were translated in the 1961 NEB as "homosexual perversion" are *malakoi* and *arsenokoitai* (discussed at length in chapter 5). They appear together only in this one passage in the New Testament. In the NRSV they are rendered as "male prostitutes, sodomites." In chapter 5, I presented a body of scholarly opinion that refutes the translation in the NEB, but I must make two additional points. First, from a scholarly perspective, it is inexcusable to insert words, from another source, that were not in the original text of the catechism. Second, from a Christian perspective it is inexcusable to create a mid-twentieth-century rendition of the catechism that appears to condemn all same-sex relations when that condemnation is not present in the sixteenth-century original. The 1989 translation of the Heidelberg Catechism published by the Reformed Church in America used the 1 Corinthians passage also, but in a footnote acknowledged that there was no word in the original text of the Heidelberg Catechism that corresponded to the phrase "homosexual perversion." Unfortunately, it is the earlier translation of the Heidelberg of 1962, without any footnote, that appears in our *Book of Confessions*. The confessions included in the Presbyterian *Book of Confessions* were chosen soon after the 1962 edition of the Heidelberg was published, and that version was chosen as the newest available.

The authors of the Heidelberg Catechism, Answer 87, did not intend that it be based on a quotation from a single biblical text. Note that the other biblical texts cited in the margin of the catechism (Eph. 5:5, 1 John 3:14–15, Gal. 5:21) focus in quite different directions from the New English Bible version of 1 Corinthians 6:9–10. Ephesians 5:5 reads, "For be very sure of this: no one given to fornication or indecency, or the greed which makes an idol of gain, has any share in the kingdom of Christ and of God."[29] What is most interesting in this passage is that it is not homosexuality (as some modern authors claim) but covetousness, greed, and striving for financial gain that are defined as idolatry.[30] First John 3:14–15 says, "for everyone who hates his brother is a murderer, and no murderer, as you know, has eternal life dwelling within him." The focus is on the sin of lacking love for one's brothers. Galatians 5:21 has a long list of sins, including "quarrels, a contentious temper, envy, fits of rage, selfish ambitions." On the basis of these four biblical texts in the margin, one could hardly argue that Answer 87 was meant to focus on homosexuality.

I wondered if perhaps the word translated as "indecency" in Ephesians 5:5 in the NEB might have supported the insertion of a reference to homosexuality. So I checked the Greek text on which the NEB was based.[31] The Greek word is *akathartos*, which, according to Liddell and Scott's *Greek-English Lexicon,* meant "uncleanness," as of a wound, moral depravity, or ceremonial impurity.[32] There is no suggestion of an application specifically to same-sex practice. I checked Ephesians 5:5 in various translations. The Geneva Bible of 1560, which could conceivably have influenced the Heidelberg Catechism of 1563, rendered *akathartos* as "unclean person."[33] The RSV and the NRSV use the word "impure" in this place. In no instance is any application to same-sex practice indicated.

So what should we conclude? From this initial investigation, it would seem that the *Book of Confessions* contains a serious flaw in the form of a very unfortunate and inaccurate insertion. It appears that some translator(s), imbued with the general 1960s American assumption that homosexuality is inherently perverse, took the liberty of assigning what Ephesians calls the sin of "impurity" not to us all, as the catechism intends, but only to one specific group of people. In the Heidelberg Catechism there is not even a word on which one could hang this prejudice. The condemnation of homosexuality is not an essential teaching of our *Book of Confessions.* Indeed, except for this inaccurate insertion, there is no mention of homosexuality at all.

One of the difficulties of translating any text is to use language that is faithful to the intent of the original and yet meaningful in our present cultural context. Unfortunately, our contemporary biases—the ones that we usually do not think to question—can influence a contemporary rendition of an older text. In this case, the Heidelberg Catechism found in the Presbyterian Church (U.S.A.) *Book of Confessions* is flawed by an inaccurate and unjustified insertion in Answer 87. The fact that this error condemns a whole class of church members makes it all the more grievous.

Principles of Our *Book of Order*

Like the *Book of Confessions*, the Presbyterian *Book of Order* embodies a trajectory toward ever-greater inclusiveness of people. The *Book of Order* stipulates that we should not deny membership with its full rights and privileges to anyone for "any other reason not related to profession of faith."[34]

The Articles of Agreement, the basis for the 1983 reunion of American Presbyterians, north and south, added four important new chapters to the *Book of Order*, none of which had been in the book of government of either of the predecessor denominations. These new chapters present the basic principles by which Presbyterians have governed and wish to govern themselves. Those principles point in the direction of increasing inclusiveness.

Chapter 3, "The Church and Its Mission," makes this principle of inclusiveness very clear. It calls the church "to a new openness to its own membership . . . becoming in fact as well as in faith a community of women and men of all ages, races, and conditions, and by providing for inclusiveness as a visible sign of the new humanity."[35] Chapter 4, "The Church and Its Unity," makes inclusiveness even more explicit:

> The Presbyterian Church (U.S.A.) shall give full expression to the rich diversity within its membership and shall provide means which will assure a greater inclusiveness leading to wholeness in its emerging life. Persons of all racial ethnic groups, different ages, both sexes, various disabilities, diverse geographical areas, different theological positions consistent with the Reformed tradition, as well as different marital conditions (married, single, widowed, or divorced) shall be guaranteed full participation and access to representation in the decision making of the church.[36]

This paragraph represents repentance for the previous explicit exclusion of people of color, women, and those who are divorced. It also evidences our increasing awareness that we have often functionally excluded from leadership people who are young, people with disabilities, people who are unmarried, and those who are not from our geographic region, or who do not fit with our particular school of theology.

This paragraph will be even more complete when it is amended to include the phrase, "different sexual orientations."

Prior to the insertion of a provision, now known as G-6.0106b (which I discuss at length below), which was intended to prohibit the ordination of gay and lesbian people to office in the church, the *Book of Order* had a perfectly adequate and appropriate definition of the qualifications for church officer: "In addition to possessing the necessary gifts and abilities, natural and acquired, those who undertake particular ministries should be persons of strong faith, dedicated discipleship, and love of Jesus Christ as Savior and Lord. Their manner of life should be a demonstration of the Christian gospel in the church and the world."[37] I know many LGBT people who qualify for leadership according to those criteria.

A Flaw in the *Book of Order*

In 1993 the Presbyterian General Assembly declared a three-year period of study regarding homosexuality. As the end of the three years drew near, the approaching 1996 assembly in Albuquerque received fifty-one overtures relating to ordination of gay and lesbian people. These overtures were assigned to a fifty-member assembly Committee on Ordination and Human Sexuality. The committee held a day of open hearings. A crowd of 1,000 people came to listen and 230 signed up to speak for or against ordination of people who are homosexual, although only 103 people were able to speak, because of the time limitations.[38]

The majority recommendation by thirty-one members of the committee contained three sentences:

> Those who are called to office in the church are to lead a life in obedience to Scripture and in conformity to the historic confessional standards of the church. Among these standards is the requirement to live either in fidelity within the covenant of marriage of *one man and one woman,* or *chastity* in singleness. Persons refusing to repent of any self-acknowledged practice *which the confessions call sin* shall not be ordained and/or installed as deacons, elders, or ministers of the Word and Sacrament. [emphasis added]

The majority report then noted a significant exception to the principles it had just enunciated: "It is not the intention of this committee, through this recommendation to the presbyteries, to change anything in the church's present standards and polity in relation to divorce and remarriage."

A minority report signed by the remaining nineteen members of the committee called for allowing each session and presbytery to decide whether to ordain people who are gay or lesbian.

When the amendment came to the floor, Friday, July 5, there was a forty-five-minute "informational presentation and prayerful reflection" on the majority and minority reports, followed by ninety minutes of debate. Two minutes of prayer followed and then the vote. The final vote approving the majority report was 313 for, 236 against, with no abstentions—57 percent for and 43 percent against.[39]

James D. Anderson, a gay Presbyterian, noted that

the original version of this amendment came from the Assembly Committee on Ordination and Human Sexuality with the phrase "marriage of one man and one woman." On the floor of the assembly, this was changed to "marriage of a man and a woman," in an attempt to circumvent clear prohibitions of divorce in the words of Jesus and in the confessions. It was thought that "a" rather than "one" would permit heterosexuals to continue to enjoy as many spouses as they wish, as long as they engage in their serial marriages one at a time. In contrast, lesbian and gay folks are held to a quite different standard. "We are not allowed even a single life-long partner. Such is the morality of apartheid."[40]

Amendment B, as the three-sentence statement approved by the assembly was known, was sent to the presbyteries as a potential change in the *Constitution*. During the debates in the presbyteries, the text of Amendment B proved to be less than clear. Practically, what does "chastity in singleness" mean? What exactly are the practices that the confessions call sin?

But while the text was not clear, almost everyone knew that the *intent* of Amendment B was to find some sort of theological basis to bar people who are gay and lesbian from being ordained. Despite the ambiguity of Amendment B, by spring 1997, out of 172 presbyteries, 97 voted yes, 74 voted no, and 1 took no action. Amendment B was thus approved and became G-6.0106b in the *Book of Order*. Of all the individuals voting in presbyteries, a bare majority of 50.69 percent voted for Amendment B, and 48.91 percent against it. With this action, the majority felt that they had effectively barred people who are homosexual from ordained office in the Presbyterian Church. It was, however, only the beginning of much confusion and controversy.

Fundamental Misunderstandings

On the surface, the amendment that came to be called G-6.0106b sounds great. Of course, everyone wants their church officers "to lead a life in obedience to Scripture and in conformity to the historic confessional standards of the church." But the inaccurate assumptions about the Bible and the confessions in the second and third sentences have caused enormous problems. I will highlight two problems in particular.

The first problem is that most Presbyterians incorrectly assume that "chastity" as it is used in the amendment means celibacy. The moderator of the assembly committee that produced Amendment B, declared that "chastity" meant "restraint from engaging in sexual intercourse outside the bonds of marriage between a man and a woman."[41] However, the committee's report made the *Book of Confessions* the basis for its judgments. In the *Book of Confessions*, chastity describes a responsible quality of life that applies to any Christian, married or single. Thus, chastity did not always mean sexual abstinence.

Since the Presbyterian *Book of Confessions* is the source referred to in the amendment, the definition of "chastity" should be taken from the context and use of the word there. Because all of the references to "chastity" in the *Book of Confessions* have application to both single and married people, "celibacy" cannot be the meaning, as the following selections from the *Book of Confessions* demonstrate [emphases added]:

Book of Confessions, 4.108, from the Heidelberg Catechism

Q. 108. What does the seventh commandment teach us?

A. That all *unchastity* is condemned by God, and that we should therefore detest it from the heart, and live *chaste* and disciplined lives, whether in holy wedlock or in single life.

Q. 109. Does God forbid nothing more than adultery and such gross sins in this commandment?

A. Since both our body and soul are a temple of the Holy Spirit, it is his will that we keep both pure and holy. Therefore he forbids all *unchaste* actions, gestures, words, thoughts, desires and whatever may excite another person to them.

Book of Confessions, 7.248, from the Westminster Larger Catechism

Q.   138. What are the duties required in the Seventh Commandment?

A.   The duties required in the Seventh Commandment are: *chastity* in body, mind, affections, words, and behavior, and the preservation of it in ourselves and others; watchfulness over the eyes and all the senses; temperance, keeping of *chaste* company, modesty in apparel, marriage by those that have not the gift of continency, conjugal love, and cohabitation; diligent labor in our callings; shunning of all occasions of uncleanness and resisting temptations thereunto.

Book of Confessions, 7.249, from the Westminster Larger Catechism

Q.   139. What are the sins forbidden in the Seventh Commandment?

A.   The sins forbidden in the Seventh Commandment, besides the neglect of the duties required, are: adultery, fornication, rape, incest, sodomy,[42] and all unnatural lusts; all unclean imaginations, thoughts, purposes, and affections; all corrupt or filthy communications, or listening thereunto; wanton looks, impudent or light behavior, immodest apparel, prohibiting of lawful, and dispensing with unlawful marriages; allowing, tolerating, keeping of stews, and resorting to them; entangling vows of single life, undue delay of marriage; having more wives or husbands than one at the same time; unjust divorce or desertion; idleness, gluttony, drunkenness, *unchaste* company; lascivious songs, books, pictures, dancings, stage-plays, all other provocations to, or acts of, uncleanness either in ourselves or others.

Chastity is a very important concept in the *Book of Confessions*. It asks that we all live our sexual lives with a responsible modesty. Chastity is compatible with "conjugal love" according to the Westminster Larger Catechism. Furthermore, in every instance in these excerpts from the *Book of Confessions* chastity applies to all people, single or married, and thus cannot be a synonym for celibacy.

The second problem, perhaps more important, is that the amendment is based on false assumptions about what exactly "the confessions call sin." In fact, all of us commit acts "which the confessions call sin," and we are not repentant either, since we no longer regard as sins many things that were forbidden in earlier times and circumstances.

The confessions are historical documents that reflect not only general biblical principles, but also the ethical standards of the time and culture in which they were written. General ignorance of the content of the confessions made it possible for Presbyterians to appear to honor the confessions without actually understanding or applying them to their daily lives. If the third sentence of G-6.0106b is taken literally, "Persons refusing to repent of any self-acknowledged practice which the confessions call sin shall not be ordained and/or installed as deacons, elders, or ministers of the Word and Sacrament," then *no* Presbyterian can be ordained or installed as deacon, elder, or minister of the Word and Sacrament.

Several examples may be helpful to illustrate my point:

1. In the seventeenth century, as English Puritans reacted against the required celibacy of the Roman Catholic priesthood, "undue delay of marriage" was specified as a sin in the Westminster Larger Catechism. The Westminster Confession declared that it is "the duty of Christians to marry onely in the Lord."[43] The seventeenth-century English Puritan application of this principle was that "such as profess the true reformed Religion, should not marry with infidels, papists or other idolaters." In fact, the pope was branded the antichrist![44]

2. The Second Helvetic Confession mandates, "Let marriages be made with consent of the parents, or of those who take the place of parents."[45] In the sixteenth and seventeenth centuries, prearranged marriages were standard practice, often at what we would think was a very young age.

3. Most Presbyterians today do not keep a Puritan Sabbath. The Westminster Catechisms enjoin us against "profaning the day by idleness, or doing that which is in itself sinful, or by unnecessary thoughts, words, or works, about our worldly employments or recreations."[46] Were we to follow this, we could not participate in sports nor watch them on television on Sunday. Nor could we even think about the work waiting for us on Monday.

4. Few of us are repentant of our "worldly amusements." Today it would be impossible to watch television and entirely avoid images that our Puritan ancestors would have categorized as sinful "lascivious songs,

books, pictures, dancings, stageplays, and all other provocations to, or acts of, uncleanness either in ourselves or others."[47] We not only observe others, but we ourselves dress in ways that the Puritans (and our grandparents) would have thought "immodest apparel."[48] The most modest bathing suit on our beaches today would not have passed Puritan muster.

5. Even some of our worship practices violate Puritan standards. We do not consider the display of religious art to be sinful today, but it was forbidden in seventeenth-century Puritan England. The Westminster Larger Catechism designates as sin "the making of any representation of God, of all, or of any of the three Persons, either inwardly in our mind, or outwardly in any kind of image or likeness of any creature whatsoever."[49]

6. Presbyterians influenced by the charismatic movement would no doubt be surprised to discover that they are unrepentant sinners according to the confessions. The confessions demand, "Therefore, let all strange tongues keep silence in gatherings for worship, and let all things be set forth in a common language which is understood by the people gathered in that place."[50] "Prayer . . . is to be made . . . if vocal, in a known tongue."[51]

There are at least 250 sins mentioned in the *Book of Confessions*, and we all practice at least some of them in good conscience. Since most people, both in the Presbyterian Church and in other denominations, are not familiar with the sixteenth- and seventeenth-century confessions,[52] the church, in practice, bars only people who are gay or lesbian from ordination and still claims to be following our confessional tradition.

The young man who crafted the third line in G-6.0106b, "Persons refusing to repent of any self-acknowledged practice which the confessions call sin shall not be ordained and/or installed as deacons, elders, or ministers of the Word and Sacrament," believed that his sentence would mean that decisions on ethical matters in the church would be made on confessional, rather than polity grounds.[53] The result has been the exact opposite.

G-6.0106b is a nice-sounding amendment that is a theological and practical mess. Those who voted for it felt like they were standing up for the Bible and the confessions! In fact, by relying on false assumptions about the Bible and the confessions, the amendment actually distorts fundamental principles of both. Ordination of people who are homosexual can be perfectly consistent with the Bible and the confessions. It is only the biased cultural assumptions about the Bible and the confessions, as contained in the second and third sentences of the amendment, that prevent lesbian and gay people from being ordained in the church.

Reaffirming the Bible and the Principles of Our Faith

As I have shown, neither the Bible nor the confessions, properly understood, is opposed to homosexuality as such. However, many Presbyterians treat homosexuality as if it were the most important issue facing the church and the worst imaginable sin a human being can commit. Allowing three sentences in the *Book of Order* to preempt our biblical and theological tradition is a grave mistake that needs to be corrected.

The best methods of interpretation, from the Reformation on down through today, call upon us to interpret the Scripture through the lens of Jesus Christ's life and ministry. Using this method, we see clearly that Jesus and the Bible, properly understood, do not condemn people who are homosexual. In church governance, our confessions and *Book of Order* embody a trajectory of ever-greater inclusiveness. To bar gay and lesbian people from ordination and marriage is a violation of these fundamental principles of our faith. One day soon, our church will once again uphold these biblical and confessional principles by welcoming our lesbian, gay, bisexual, and transgender sisters and brothers as full and equal members in our church and society. The Holy Spirit is at work in the church. Praise God.

Notes

Preface

1. The first known use of the word "homosexual" in English was in 1892 in C. G. Chaddock's translation of Krafft-Ebing's *Psychopathia Sexualis* 3:225. While the use of the word homosexual originated in a medical context where it was linked to pathology, I show in this book that contemporary science finds no such link.

Since finishing this book I have become aware that bisexual and transgender people do not recognize themselves in the term "homosexual." It is a problem of my social location and that of the audience I am addressing that we do not yet fully understand and have not yet incorporated into our vocabulary distinctions that are essential to members of the LGBT community.

Finding the right word to describe real people who embody an array of human gender expression is difficult. We learned the importance of changing nomenclature in the civil rights struggle when identifying terms changed from "colored" to "Negro" to "black" to "African American." I am helped by the recent study by Mark D. Jordan, professor of religion at Emory University, and a gay man, in his recent book *Blessing Same-Sex Unions: The Perils of Queer Romance and the Confusions of Christian Marriage* (Chicago: University of Chicago Press, 2005), 20, where he struggles to find an appropriate term of generalization. He opts for "queer" as do most LGBT folk and many in the academic community. While "queer" has become a symbol of empowerment within the LGBT community, I do not use that term because for the heterosexual community I am addressing "queer" still sounds pejorative.

This book is meant to support full inclusion in the church and society of all LGBT people. When I use the word "homosexual" I mean it in the way that it is used in the press, and in church documents, as a general term for people who self-identify as not being in the majority population of those who think of themselves as heterosexual. Indeed, I am primarily addressing a church culture of people who think that everyone is heterosexual and that those who express their sexuality in any other way are acting against their nature. That is a myth that I am trying to correct.

I hope that in a few years those of us in the heterosexual community, including myself, will become more skilled in describing the realities of the LGBT community. I long ago learned that "man" was not a word that included women. I hope to be as sensitive to appropriate terms in the LGBT community in the future. My desire is that this book will help to erase any pejorative connotation that clings to words describing people whose sexual orientation is different than the majority. The time will come when all people are recognized as created by God and acceptable just as they have been created.

2. Beginning in 2004, the term has been extended to two years.

3. Addison Hardie Leitch.

4. In this chapter and the next, I present research I did, some of which has already been published in my earlier book *Reading the Bible and the Confessions: The Presbyterian Way* (Louisville, KY: Geneva Press, 1999).

Chapter 1: Studying Homosexuality for the First Time

1. In Presbyterian government the session is the governing body of a congregation composed of elected elders and the ministers of Word and Sacrament.

2. More Light is a Presbyterian designation for a congregation that is willing to elect qualified lesbian, gay, bisexual, and transgender persons to all offices in the church. Other denominations have similar movements with different names.

3. In Presbyterian polity, deacons are ordained to a ministry of service. They have no governance or other ministry function. Elders are members who have been ordained to a ministry of governance and general spiritual oversight in collaboration with the pastors, who are ministers of Word and Sacrament.

4. There was a cost, however. The congregation lost at least ten members and $40,000 in pledges from people who were uncomfortable with the study.

5. Much of the material in this introduction has been previously published in Jack Rogers, *Confessions of a Conservative Evangelical,* 2nd ed. (Louisville, KY: Geneva Press, 2001).

6. For a historical sketch of this period see Jack Rogers, *Claiming the Center: Churches and Conflicting Worldviews* (Louisville, KY: Westminster John Knox, 1995), 29–39.

7. For a detailed discussion of the Old Princeton interpretation of Scripture, see Jack B. Rogers and Donald K. McKim, *The Authority and Interpretation of the Bible: An Historical Approach* (San Francisco: Harper & Row, 1979), chapters 5 and 6. (A 1999 reprint edition, with a new epilogue, is available from Wipf & Stock Publishers, 150 West Broadway, Eugene, OR 97401.)

8. Reformed is the theological name for that Protestant tradition with roots in the Calvinism that began in what we now call Switzerland. It is one of the Reformation strands, along with Lutheranism, Anglicanism, and Anabaptism.

9. Jack Bartlett Rogers, *Scripture in the Westminster Confession: A Problem of Historical Interpretation for American Presbyterianism* (Grand Rapids: Eerdmans, 1967).

10. G. C. Berkouwer, *Holy Scripture,* trans. and ed. Jack Rogers (Grand Rapids: Eerdmans, 1975).

11. See George Marsden, *Reforming Fundamentalism: Fuller Seminary and the New Evangelicalism* (Grand Rapids: Eerdmans, 1987).

12. Richard N. Ostling, "Evangelicals' Platform Shows Complex Political Profile," *Pasadena Star-News*, January 28, 2005, D5. University of Akron political scientist John C. Green asserts that the National Association of Evangelicals represents evangelicalism's pragmatic center. For Green, the progressive, or left, wing of evangelicalism is represented, for example, by Jim Wallis of *Sojourners* magazine in his new book *God's Politics: Why the Right Gets It Wrong and the Left Doesn't Get It* (San Francisco: Harper & Row, 2005), and leaders of the right wing include not only Jerry Falwell and Pat Robertson but James Dobson of Focus on the Family and Southern Baptist executive Richard Land. This extreme right would more properly be known as fundamentalists.

13. *The Fundamentalist Phenomenon: The Resurgence of Conservative Christianity*, ed. Jerry Falwell with Ed Dobson and Ed Hindson (Garden City, NY: Doubleday & Co., 1981).

14. George Marsden in *Fundamentalism and American Culture: The Shaping of Twentieth-Century Evangelicalism: 1870–1925* (New York: Oxford University Press, 1980), 4, describes fundamentalism as "militantly anti-modernist Protestant evangelicalism."

15. See Jack Rogers, "Inerrancy," in *A New Handbook of Christian Theology*, ed. Donald W. Musser and Joseph L. Price (Nashville: Abingdon Press, 1992), 254–56.

16. Harold Lindsell, *The Battle for the Bible* (Grand Rapids: Zondervan, 1976).

17. Jack Rogers, ed., *Biblical Authority* (Waco, TX: Word Books, 1977). My article was "The Church Doctrine of Biblical Authority," pp. 15–46.

18. Rogers and McKim, *The Authority and Interpretation of the Bible*.

19. See, for example, John D. Woodbridge, *Biblical Authority: A Critique of the Rogers/McKim Proposal* (Grand Rapids: Zondervan, 1982).

20. The editor of *Christianity Today*, Kenneth Kantzer, referred to me as a "black beast."

21. The United Presbyterian Church in the United States of America was the result of a merger in 1958 of the United Presbyterian Church of North America and the Presbyterian Church in the U.S.A.

22. "The Church and Homosexuality," *Blue Book I, 190th General Assembly (1978) of the United Presbyterian Church in the United States of America, San Diego, California, May 16–24, 1978*, pp. D-1-D-201.

23. For further discussion, see "Pluralism and Policy in Presbyterian Views of Scripture," by Jack B. Rogers and Donald K. McKim, in *The Confessional Mosaic: Presbyterians and Twentieth-Century Theology*, ed. Milton J Coalter, John M. Mulder, and Louis B. Weeks (Louisville, KY: Westminster/John Knox Press, 1990), 37–58.

24. *Minutes* of the General Assembly, UPCUSA, 1978b, 61–62.

25. Tom Gillespie, chair of the assembly committee, announced that the committee was recommending that the assembly "not exercise its right to render a constitutional interpretation." He said that to do so would call into question the

constitutional rights of the presbyteries in the ordination process. The committee proposed "rather, that it offer the 'definitive guidance' requested." *Church and Society* 68, no. 5 (May-June 1978): 22–24.

26. See *The Constitution of the Presbyterian Church (U.S.A.), Part II, Book of Order, 2003–2004* (Louisville, KY: Office of the General Assembly, 2003), G-14.0207 and G-14.0405.

27. "Report of the Committee on Pluralism in the Church to the 190th General Assembly (1978) of the United Presbyterian Church in the United States of America," *Minutes*, 1978, Part I, p. 293.

28. For a discussion of the three mandates of the task force see "Pluralism and Policy in Presbyterian Views of Scripture," by Jack B. Rogers and Donald K. McKim, in *The Confessional Mosaic*, 49–52.

29. For the result, see *Presbyterian Use and Understanding of Scripture, a Position Statement of the General Assembly, Presbyterian Church (U.S.A.)* (New York and Atlanta: Office of the General Assembly, 1983), n.p.

30. A booklet named for and containing the two reports was published in Louisville by the Office of the General Assembly of the Presbyterian Church (U.S.A.) in 1992. Both the PCUS report, "Presbyterian Understanding and Use of Holy Scripture," and the UPCUSA report, "Biblical Authority and Interpretation," are printed in this booklet, published by the Office of the General Assembly in 1992 and available from Presbyterian Distribution Service, Louisville, KY, as #OGA-92-003.

31. Jeffrey S. Siker, ed., *Homosexuality in the Church: Both Sides of the Debate* (Louisville, KY: Westminster John Knox, 1994), 195–208, provides an appendix with the relevant documents. He includes earlier statements of the Episcopal Church and the Southern Baptist Convention as well. The definitive statement of the Roman Catholic Church to that time is found on 39–47.

32. The Coalition now has a variety of objectives, all concerned with reform and renewal of the Presbyterian Church in a generally conservative direction.

33. "Correction," *Presbyterian Outlook*, vol. 179, no. 8 (March 3, 1997), 2. Five percent, or 620 congregations, undertook the study, but in half of these only the session studied the matter. Thus only 2.5 percent of the congregations conducted a congregational study.

34. Personal conversation, but in a public setting.

35. *Book of Order*, The Form of Government, G-6.0106b. This section is popularly referred to as G-6.0106b.

36. See J. Gordon Melton, *The Churches Speak on Homosexuality: Official Statements from Religious Bodies and Ecumenical Organizations* (Detroit: Gale Research, 1991). Siker, ed., *Homosexuality in the Church*, "Appendix: Selected Denominational Statements on Homosexuality," 195–208, cites recent statements by the Episcopal Church, the Evangelical Lutheran Church in America, the Presbyterian Church (U.S.A.), the Southern Baptist Convention, the United Church of Christ, and the United Methodist Church.

37. The definition of "sodomy" has changed over time. In the Middle Ages it referred to any form of sexual expression that was not open to procreation. Then it focused on anal intercourse. Until the twentieth century, such sexual expression was viewed as wrong and often made illegal, whether by heterosexual or homosexual couples. Then the law was narrowed in the U.S. to apply to homosexuals only. See Alan A. Brash, *Facing Our Differences: The Churches and Their Gay and Lesbian Members* (Geneva, Switzerland: WCC Publications, 1995), 37.

38. *Boston Globe*, November 18, 2003. See http://www.boston.com/news/specials/gay_marriage/gallery/timeline/ recorded on March 28, 2005.

39. *Boston Globe*, January 20, 2005. See http://www.boston.com/news/specials/gay_marriage/gallery/timeline?pg=2. Recorded on March 28, 2005.

40. *Boston Globe*, February 24, 2004. See http://boston.com/news/specials/gay_marriage/gallery/timeline?pg=10. Recorded on March 28, 2005.

41. The pastor of a large Presbyterian Church wrote to me in those terms. Alan Keyes, a candidate for United States Senate, declared that the definition of marriage "will determine the life and death of the freedom and morality of our country" (cited in Emma Schwartz and Kathleen Hennessey, "A Marriage-Minded Protest," *Los Angeles Times*, October 16, 2004, A8).

42. Dr. James Dobson, *Focus on the Family Newsletter* (April 2004), and read on his March 24, 2004, radio broadcast, cited in Jeff Lutes, "A False Focus on My Family" (Lynchburg, VA: Soulforce, 2005) at www.DearDrDobson.com, January 24, 2005.

43. See *Book of Order*, G-5.0202: "An active member is entitled to all the rights and privileges of the church, including the *right* to . . . vote and hold office." It is that *eligibility* for office that we are unconstitutionally denying to our faithful gay and lesbian members.

Chapter 2: A Pattern of Misusing the Bible to Justify Oppression

1. Jack Rogers, "Should the United Presbyterian Church Ordain Homosexuals?" (Boston: The Case Study Institute, 1976), 18.

2. Robert A. J. Gagnon, in Dan O. Via and Robert A. J. Gagnon, *Homosexuality and the Bible: Two Views* (Minneapolis: Fortress Press, 2003), 44–47. For Gagnon's argument in more detail, see Robert A. J. Gagnon, *The Bible and Homosexual Practice: Texts and Hermeneutics* (Nashville: Abingdon Press, 2000), 442–52; Thomas E. Schmidt, *Straight and Narrow: Compassion and Clarity in the Homosexuality Debate* (Downers Grove, IL: InterVarsity Press, 1995), 26–27; Christopher Seitz, "Sexuality and Scripture's Plain Sense: The Christian Community and the Law of God," in *Homosexuality, Science, and the "Plain Sense" of Scripture*, ed. David L. Balch (Grand Rapids: Eerdmans, 2000), 182; Ray S. Anderson, "Homosexuality and the Ministry of the Church: Theological and Pastoral Considerations," in *More Than a Single Issue: Theological Considerations concerning the Ordination of Practising People Who Are Homosexual*, ed. Murray A. Rae and Graham Redding (P.O. Box 504, Hindmarsh SA 5007: Australian Theological Forum, 2000), 75.

3. John D'Emilio and Estelle B. Freedman, *Intimate Matters: A History of Sexuality in America* (New York: Harper & Row, 1988), xvi: "Whites imposed on blacks an image of a beastlike sexuality to justify both the rape of black women and the lynching of black men."

4. *Authorized Version of the English Bible*, 1611, commonly known as the King James Version. This translation of the Bible was the standard one in English from the time of colonization until the late 1950s.

5. 19:15, cited in Stephen R. Haynes, *Noah's Curse: The Biblical Justification of American Slavery* (New York: Oxford University Press, 2002), 225n14.

6. Haynes, *Noah's Curse*, esp. chap. 2.

7. Ernest Trice Thompson, *Presbyterians in the South*, vol. 1, *1607–1861* (Richmond: John Knox Press, 1963), 530. Some of the material in this chapter can be found as well in my book *Reading the Bible and the Confessions: The Presbyterian Way* (Louisville, KY: Geneva Press, 1999).

8. James Oscar Farmer Jr., *The Metaphysical Confederacy: James Henley Thornwell and the Synthesis of Southern Values* (Macon, GA: Mercer University Press, 1986), 222, and Thompson, 1:536.

9. *Address of the General Assembly of the Presbyterian Church in the Confederate States of America to All the Churches of Jesus Christ Throughout the Earth, Adopted Unanimously at the Organization of the General Assembly in Augusta, Ga., December, 1861* (n.p.: Published by order of the Assembly, n.d.), 5.

10. Ibid., 11.

11. Ibid., 15.

12. Ibid., 14.

13. Ibid., 11.

14. Ibid.

15. Ibid., 12.

16. Ibid., 15.

17. Ibid.

18. Cited in Eugene D. Genovese, "An Uncertain Trumpet: How Christians in the South Sought to Reconcile Slavery with Scripture," in *Books & Culture*, January/February 1999, 36. In December 1861, the Reverend J. Henry Smith of North Carolina had used almost the same words, saying: "If we fail, the progress of civilization will be thrown back a century."

19. S.v. "Dabney, Robert Lewis," in Randall Balmer and John R. Fitzmier, *The Presbyterians*, Denominations in America 5, ed. Henry Warner Bowden (Westport, CT: Greenwood Press, 1993), 147.

20. Ernest Trice Thompson, *Presbyterians in the South*, vol. 2, *1861–1890* (Richmond: John Knox Press, 1973), 200.

21. Thompson, 2:200.

22. Cited in Haynes, *Noah's Curse*, 71, quoting Dabney, "A Defense of Virginia and through Her of the South, in Recent and Pending Contests against the Sectional Party," 1867.

23. Thompson, 2:217.

24. Cited in Thomas Cary Johnson, *The Life and Letters of Robert Lewis Dabney* (Richmond: Presbyterian Committee of Publication, 1903), 320.

25. "Ecclesiastical Relation of Negroes," *Speech of Rev. Robert L. Dabney, in the Synod of Virginia, Nov. 9, 1867; Against The Ecclesiastical Equality of Negro Preachers in Our Church, and Their Right to Rule Over White Christians* (Richmond: Printed at the Office of the "Boys and Girls' Monthly," 1868), 8. Cf. Thompson, 2:218.

26. "Ecclesiastical Relation," 8.

27. Ibid., 10.

28. Ibid., 8.

29. Ibid.

30. Thompson, 2:218–219.

31. Robert L. Dabney, "Anti-Biblical Theories of Rights," *Presbyterian Quarterly* 2, no. 2 (July 1888): 215–42, 219. Hereafter cited as "Rights."

32. Dabney, "Rights," 232–33.

33. Ibid., 223–24.

34. Cited in Genovese, "An Uncertain Trumpet," 36.

35. D'Emilio and Freedman, *Intimate Matters*, 28: "Western culture had traditionally feared the sexual voraciousness of women. As the 'weaker vessel,' woman supposedly had less mastery over her passions and had to be carefully controlled."

36. Cited in *Minutes*, PC(USA), 1987, 643.

37. Betty A. DeBerg, *Ungodly Women: Gender and the First Wave of American Fundamentalism* (Minneapolis: Fortress Press, 1990), 20.

38. Cited in DeBerg, *Ungodly Women*, 20.

39. *Extract from Minutes of the General Assembly*, PCUSA, 1803–1811, 310, cited in Karen (Bear) Ride Scott, "Expanding the Horizons of Ministry: Women of the Cloth in the Presbyterian Church, U.S.A." (DMin diss. project, San Francisco Theological Seminary, 1990), 84.

40. Lois A. Boyd and R. Douglas Brackenridge, *Presbyterian Women in America: Two Centuries of a Quest for Status*, Contributions to the Study of Religion 9, A Publication of the Presbyterian Historical Society (Westport, CT: Greenwood Press, 1983), 6.

41. Ronald W. Hogeland, "Charles Hodge, The Association of Gentlemen and Ornamental Womanhood: 1825–1855," *Journal of Presbyterian History* 53, no. 3 (Fall 1975): 245.

42. John W. Stewart, "Charles Hodge Revisited," *Princeton Seminary Bulletin* 18, no. 3 (November 1997): 287. An abridged edition of Hodge's *Systematic Theology*, edited by Edward N. Gross, was published in 1988 by Baker Book House in Grand Rapids.

43. Cited in Hogeland, "Charles Hodge," 247–48.

44. Dabney, "Rights," 223.

45. Ibid., 219.

46. Cited in Boyd and Brackenridge, *Presbyterian Women in America*, 208.

47. Cited in Boyd and Brackenridge, *Presbyterian Women in America*, 217–18.

48. Ibid., 212.

49. Jack B. Rogers and Donald K. McKim, *The Authority and Interpretation of the Bible: An Historical Approach* (San Francisco: Harper & Row, 1979), 242–43.

50. Cited in Rogers and McKim, *The Authority and Interpretation of the Bible*, 293.

51. Ibid., 235–42.

52. Ibid., 242.

53. Farmer, *Metaphysical Confederacy*, 138.

54. Ibid., 134–35.

55. See Morton H. Smith, *Studies in Southern Presbyterian Theology* (Amsterdam: Jacob Van Campen, 1962), 202 and 205. Smith, writing as a mid-twentieth-century Southerner, admired Dabney and agreed with his argument regarding slavery.

56. Cited in Rogers and McKim, *The Authority and Interpretation of the Bible*, 293.

57. William B. Gravely, "Christian Abolitionism," in Ronald C. White Jr. and C. Howard Hopkins, *The Social Gospel: Religion and Reform in Changing America* (Philadelphia: Temple University Press, 1976), 18. In contrast to others who called for the gradual elimination of slavery, abolitionists called for its immediate end.

58. Aileen S. Kraditor, *Means and Ends in American Abolitionism: Garrison and His Critics on Strategy and Tactics, 1834–1850* (New York: Pantheon Books, 1967), 41 and 83.

59. John R. McKivigan, *The War against Proslavery Religion: Abolitionism and the Northern Churches, 1830–1865* (Ithaca, NY: Cornell University Press, 1984), 31.

60. Ibid., 20.

61. Gravely, "Christian Abolitionism," 18.

62. McKivigan, *War against Proslavery Religion*, 13.

63. Ibid., 58.

Chapter 3: A Breakthrough in Understanding the Word of God

1. For further discussion, see Jack Rogers, *Claiming the Center: Churches and Conflicting Worldviews* (Louisville, KY: Westminster John Knox, 1995), 15–17.

2. Ibid., 34–35.

3. For the full and original wordings of these "essentials," see *The Presbyterian Enterprise: Sources of American Presbyterian History*, ed. Maurice W. Armstrong, Lefferts A. Loetscher, and Charles A. Anderson (Philadelphia: Westminster Press, 1956), 281. The nondenominational fundamentalist movement took these five essentials and modified them to make #2 the deity of Christ, and #5 the premillennial return of Christ. These came to be called the "five fundamentals."

4. According to usual parliamentary rules, the person who is moderating, or chairing, a meeting cannot make a motion. Therefore, Erdman, following proper

procedure, turned the chair, or the moderating of the meeting, over to his vice-moderator, and Erdman was then, himself, permitted to make a motion.

5. See, further, Jack B. Rogers and Donald K. McKim, *The Authority and Interpretation of the Bible: An Historical Approach* (San Francisco: Harper & Row, 1979), 366–67.

6. Jack Rogers, *Reading the Bible and the Confessions: The Presbyterian Way* (Louisville, KY: Geneva Press, 1999), 92–98.

7. The group comprised approximately 13 percent of the ministers in the church. Many of them were pastors of large churches, who thus exercised considerable influence. See Charles E. Quick, "A Statistical Analysis of the Signers of the Auburn Affirmation," *Journal of Presbyterian History* 43, no. 3 (Fall 1965): 182–96, esp. 183 and 193.

8. "An Affirmation designed to safeguard the unity and liberty of the Presbyterian Church in the United States of America," Auburn, NY, n.d., p. 6, cited in Rogers, *Reading the Bible and the Confessions*, 96.

9. Donald McKim, *Westminster Dictionary of Theological Terms* (Louisville, KY: Westminster John Knox, 1996), s.v. "Neo-orthodoxy."

10. For a recent exposition and appraisal of the thought of Barth, Brunner, and five other theologians usually designated as neo-orthodox, see Douglas John Hall, *Remembered Voices: Reclaiming the Legacy of "Neo-Orthodoxy"* (Louisville, KY: Westminster John Knox, 1998).

11. McKim, *Dictionary*, s.v. "Kierkegaardian."

12. *Presbyterian Understanding and Use of Holy Scripture [and] Biblical Authority and Interpretation* (Louisville, KY: Office of the General Assembly, 1992), 38–44.

13. See chapter 1, p. 9, for theologians identified with neo-orthodoxy.

14. W. Eugene March, "'Biblical Theology,' Authority and the Presbyterians," *Journal of Presbyterian History* 59, no. 2 (Summer 1981): 118.

15. "Presbyterian scholars such as G. Ernest Wright, Floyd V. Filson, James D. Smart, John Wick Bowman, John A. Mackay, Joseph Haroutunian, Otto Piper, Arnold Rhodes, John Bright, Donald G. Miller, Balmer H. Kelly, and others, led the way in the '40s and '50s in advocating a new 'biblical theology'" (ibid., 118).

16. Ibid., 118–19.

17. Ibid., 119.

18. Ibid., 121.

19. Ibid., 121–22.

20. E. T. Thompson, *Presbyterians in the South*, vol. 3, *1890–1972* (Richmond: John Knox Press, 1973), 336.

21. Ibid., 3:338.

22. Ibid., 3:339.

23. Ibid., 3:539.

24. Ibid., 3:540.

25. "Report of the Ad Interim Committee on a Biblical Study of the Position of Women in the Church," *Minutes*, PCUS, 1956, 141.

26. *Book of Confessions*, 6.009, cited in "Report . . . Women," *Minutes, PCUS,* 1956, 139.

27. "Report . . . Women," *Minutes, PCUS, 1956, 139.*

28. *Minutes,* PCUSA, 1929, cited in James G. Emerson Jr., "The Remarriage of Divorced Persons in the United Presbyterian Church of the United States of America" (PhD diss., Divinity School of the University of Chicago, 1959), 125.

29. *Minutes,* PCUSA, 1930, 86–87.

30. Ibid., 87.

31. Ibid., 88.

32. James G. Emerson Jr., *Divorce, the Church, and Remarriage* (Philadelphia: Westminster Press, 1961), 127.

33. *Minutes,* PCUS, 1938, 110. Cf. Thompson, 3:516.

34. *Minutes,* PCUS, 1946, 104.

35. *Minutes,* PCUS, 1953, 89.

36. Ibid., 90.

37. Ibid.

38. Ibid.

39. *Minutes,* PCUS, 1959, 68–70; Thompson, 3:518–19.

40. *Minutes,* PCUS, 1959, 69; *Book of Confessions,* 6.137–6.138.

41. Eric Mount Jr. and Johanna W. H. Bos, "Scripture on Sexuality: Shifting Authority," *Journal of Presbyterian History* 59, no. 2 (Summer 1981): 224.

42. See especially John 7:53–8:11, the story of the woman taken in adultery.

43. Jack Rogers, "The Day before Christmas," in *On Speech and Speakers: An Anthology of Writings and Models,* ed. H. Bruce Kendall and Charles J. Stewart (New York: Holt, Rinehart & Winston, 1968), 233.

44. Rogers, "The Day before Christmas," 234.

45. Jack Rogers, "Biblical Authority and Confessional Change," *Journal of Presbyterian History* 59, no. 2 (Summer 1981): 136–37.

46. For a complete list of the committee at all stages, see *Report of the Special Committee on a Brief Contemporary Statement of Faith* (Philadelphia: Office of the General Assembly, 1965), 10.

47. Rogers, "Biblical Authority and Confessional Change," 142–43.

48. Edward A. Dowey Jr., *A Commentary on the Confession of 1967 and An Introduction to the Book of Confessions* (Philadelphia: Westminster Press, 1968), 40–41.

49. *Book of Confessions,* 9.44.

50. "A Declaration of Faith (Presbyterian Church in the United States)" in *The Proposed Book of Confessions with Related Documents.* Approved by the 116th General Assembly and Recommended to the Presbyteries for Their Advice and Consent (Atlanta: Presbyterian Church in the United States, 1976), chapter 6, lines 65–67. The declaration did not receive the necessary three-quarters vote to become part of the PCUS *Constitution,* but it was used widely in the congregations.

51. Declaration of Faith, chapter 2, lines 122–25.

52. Jack Rogers, "The Kenyon Case," in *Women and Men in Ministry*, ed. Roberta Hestenes (Pasadena, CA: Fuller Theological Seminary, 1985), 148.

53. For a brief discussion of the Adopting Act of 1729, see Rogers, *Reading the Bible and the Confessions*, 91–92.

54. Rogers, "Kenyon Case," 148.

55. Ibid., 157–58.

56. Ibid., 150.

57. *Book of Confessions*, 9.44.

58. Rogers, "Kenyon Case," 150.

59. Jack Rogers, *Presbyterian Creeds: A Guide to the Book of Confessions* (Louisville, KY: Westminster John Knox Press, 1991), 231–32.

60. *Book of Confessions*, 10.3, lines 29–32.

61. *Book of Confessions*, 10.4, line 64.

62. *Book of Confessions*, 10.3, lines 47–51.

63. Rogers, *Presbyterian Creeds*, 268–69.

Chapter 4: Interpreting the Bible in Times of Controversy

1. I discussed these guidelines in my earlier book *Reading the Bible and the Confessions: The Presbyterian Way* (Louisville, KY: Geneva Press, 1999). Some of the material in this chapter, especially citations from the Reformed confessions, will overlap with that earlier publication.

2. *Presbyterian Understanding and Use of Holy Scripture and Biblical Authority and Interpretation* (Louisville, KY: Office of the General Assembly, 1992), preface. These two reports were gathered into one booklet with the following comment: "The two papers were written in response to the need for a common basis in a diverse church for understanding and using Scripture." Hereafter cited as Guidelines.

3. See chap. 3 for more specifics on the context of this discussion.

4. Guidelines, 41–44.

5. Ibid., 43.

6. Ibid., 51.

7. Ibid., 52.

8. Cited in *Presbyterian Understanding and Use of Holy Scripture, Position Statement Adopted by the 123rd General Assembly (1983) of the Presbyterian Church in the United States* (Louisville, KY: Office of the General Assembly, 1992), 17.

9. Guidelines, 17, The Geneva Confession of 1541.

10. Guidelines, 17, The Synod of Berne of 1528.

11. *Book of Confessions*, 3.18.

12. *BC*, 8.11.

13. *BC*, 9.29.

14. Guidelines, 18, A Declaration of Faith.

15. See the brave and painfully honest admission of a pastor, Joanna Adams, that even without intending it she caused another great pain in the Covenant Network–sponsored film "Turning Points."

16. Calvin, *Institutes of the Christian Religion* 4.16.23, cited in Jack B. Rogers and Donald K. McKim, *The Authority and Interpretation of the Bible* (San Francisco: Harper & Row, 1979), 97.

17. *BC*, 5.010.

18. *BC*, 9.29.

19. Guidelines, 12.

20. Guidelines, 11–12.

21. Guidelines, 11.

22. Richard B. Hays, "Awaiting the Redemption of Our Bodies," *Sojourners* 20 (July 1991): 18.

23. The first known use of the word "homosexual" in English was in 1892. C. G. Chaddock's translation of Krafft-Ebing's *Psychopathia Sexualis* 3:255 contained the reference to a patient, "He had been free from homo-sexual inclinations."

24. *BC*, 6.006.

25. *BC*, 6.010.

26. *BC*, 9.30.

27. Guidelines, 21.

28. For an application of this to homosexuality, see Jeffrey S. Siker, "Homosexual Christians, the Bible, and Gentile Inclusion: Confessions of a Repenting Heterosexist," in Jeffrey S. Siker, ed., *Homosexuality in the Church: Both Sides of the Debate* (Louisville, KY: Westminster John Knox Press, 1994), 187–91.

29. *BC*, 4.022.

30. *BC*, 5.010.

31. *Presbyterian Understanding and Use*, 21.

32. The recent (1962) insertion of the phrase "homosexual perversion" in the Heidelberg Catechism, Answer 87, is without historical justification, as I will show in chapter 7.

33. *BC*, 4.108.

34. *BC*, 5.246.

35. *BC*, 7.49.

36. *BC*, 7.48.

37. *BC*, 9.44–46.

38. *BC*, 9.47.

39. Ibid.

40. *BC*, 3.18.

41. *BC*, 5.010.

42. Guidelines, 20.

43. Walter Wink, "Homosexuality and the Bible," in *Homosexuality and Christian Faith: Questions of Conscience for the Churches,* ed. Walter Wink (Minneapolis: Fortress Press, 1999), 44.

44. *BC*, 6.007.

45. *BC*, 6.008.

46. *BC*, 6.175.

47. Guidelines, 22.

48. *The Oxford Dictionary of the Christian Church*, ed. F. L. Cross, 3rd ed., ed. E. A. Livingstone (Oxford: Oxford University Press, 1997), s.v. "Textual Criticism": "The belief that textual criticism has radically altered the text lying behind the traditional translations of the Bible has been one of the factors prompting the production of modern versions in recent times. . . . But the resulting changes in the text, at least so far as the NT is concerned, are by no means so fundamental as is often supposed." Cf. Eldon Jay Epp, "Ancient Texts and Versions of the New Testament," in *The New Interpreter's Bible*, vol. 8 (Nashville: Abingdon Press, 1995), 1–11.

49. Martti Nissinen, *Homoeroticism in the Biblical World: A Historical Perspective*, trans. Kirsi Stjerna (Minneapolis: Fortress Press, 1998), 43.

50. Phyllis A. Bird, "The Bible in Christian Ethical Deliberation concerning Homosexuality: Old Testament Contributions," in *Homosexuality, Science, and the "Plain Sense" of Scripture*, ed. David L. Balch (Grand Rapids: Eerdmans, 2000), 157.

51. Victor Paul Furnish, "The Bible and Homosexuality: Reading the Texts in Context," in Siker, ed., *Homosexuality in the Church*, 31.

52. *BC*, 5.010.

53. *BC*, 6.009.

54. Guidelines, 52. Guideline #1.

55. In Presbyterian government, election to office is a privilege, but eligibility for election is a *right* according to the church constitution. See *Book of Order*, G-5.0202: "An active member is entitled to all the rights and privileges of the church, including the right . . . to vote and hold office."

Chapter 5: What the Bible Says and Doesn't Say about Homosexuality

1. Richard B. Hays, "Awaiting the Redemption of Our Bodies: The Witness of Scripture concerning Homosexuality," in Jeffrey S. Siker, ed., *Homosexuality in the Church: Both Sides of the Debate* (Louisville, KY: Westminster John Knox Press, 1994), 5. Hays views homosexuality as evidence of human sinfulness, based on his reading of Romans 1. I deal with his view later in this chapter.

2. Daniel A. Helminiak, *What the Bible Really Says about Homosexuality*, millennium edition, updated and expanded (Tijaque, NM: Alamo Square Press, 2000), 46.

3. Some writers believe that the statement by the men of Sodom, "Bring them out to us, so that we may know them" (Gen. 19:5) has a homosexual connotation. That is not necessarily the case. The Hebrew word *yada*, meaning "to know," appears almost 1,000 times in the Hebrew Scriptures. It is used to refer to sexual intercourse only ten or eleven times. In each case the reference is to heterosexual intercourse. Therefore we should be cautious in attributing any homosexual connotation to it. See Don Blosser, "Why Does the Bible Divide Us? A Conversation with Scripture on Same-Gender Attraction," in *To Continue the Dialogue: Biblical Interpretation and Homosexuality*, ed. Norman Kraus (Telford, PA: Pandora Press,

2001), 121–47, cited in David G. Myers and Letha Dawson Scanzoni, *What God Has Joined Together? A Christian Case for Gay Marriage* (San Francisco: HarperSanFrancisco, 2005), 86.

4. Helminiak, *What the Bible Really Says*, 46.

5. Dale B. Martin, "*Arsenokoites* and *Malakos*: Meanings and Consequences," in Robert L. Brawley, ed., *Biblical Ethics and Homosexuality: Listening to Scripture* (Louisville, KY: Westminster John Knox Press, 1996), 129.

6. Ibid., 127.

7. Martti Nissinen, *Homoeroticism in the Biblical World: A Historical Perspective*, trans. Kirsi Stjerna (Minneapolis: Fortress Press, 1998), 48. Cf. Phyllis A. Bird, "The Bible in Christian Ethical Deliberation concerning Homosexuality: Old Testament Contributions," in *Homosexuality, Science, and the "Plain Sense" of Scripture*, ed. David L. Balch (Grand Rapids: Eerdmans, 2000), 148.

8. Choon-Leong Seow, "Textual Orientation," in Brawley, ed., *Biblical Ethics and Homosexuality* (Louisville, KY: Westminster John Knox Press, 1996), 22.

9. Ibid., 22. Cf. Helminiak, *What the Bible Really Says*, 48–49. Other Old Testament references include Isa. 1:10–17 and 3:9, Jer. 23:14, Ezek.16:49, and Zeph. 2:8–11.

10. Nissinen, *Homoeroticism*, 47.

11. Ibid., 47.

12. Bird, "The Bible in Christian Ethical Deliberation," 149–50.

13. Victor Paul Furnish, "The Bible and Homosexuality: Reading the Texts in Context," in *Homosexuality in the Church*, 20.

14. Helminiak, *What the Bible Really Says*, 52–53.

15. Furnish, "The Bible and Homosexuality," 20.

16. Bird, "The Bible in Christian Ethical Deliberation," 157.

17. Nissinen, *Homoeroticism*, 42. Cf. Bird, "The Bible in Christian Ethical Deliberation," 151.

18. Myers and Scanzoni, *What God Has Joined Together?* 90. They note that Tim and Beverly LaHaye, conservative Christians who insist that same-sex acts are an abomination, nonetheless counsel modern married couples to have intercourse during the wife's menstrual period.

19. Marion L. Soards, *Scripture and Homosexuality: Biblical Authority and the Church Today* (Louisville, KY: Westminster John Knox, 1995), 17. He says that for two reasons: "Given the historical setting and purpose of the Holiness Code in which Lev. 18:22 and 20:13 occur, and more, given that we confess in faith that Christ is the end of the law (Rom. 10:4)."

20. Brian Blount, "Reading and Understanding the New Testament on Homosexuality," in *Homosexuality and Christian Community*, ed. Choon-Leong Seow (Louisville, KY: Westminster John Knox Press, 1996), 33.

21. Ibid., 33. Blount comments regarding 1 Cor. 6:9: "Chronologically, this is Paul's first statement on this issue, and it is also his least understandable." Cf. Nissinen, *Homoeroticism*, 113.

22. Nissinen, *Homoeroticism*, 113.

23. Ibid., 115.

24. Martin, "*Arsenokoites* and *Malakos*," 119.

25. Ibid., 119.

26. Ibid., 121.

27. Ibid., 123. Martin, in the notes to his article, seems to treat these quoted words as a general claim made by antigay scholars.

28. Nissinen, *Homoeroticism*, 118.

29. Martin, "*Arsenokoites* and *Malakos*," 128–29.

30. Nissinen, *Homoeroticism*, 114.

31. Furnish, "The Bible and Homosexuality," 19. The OT references in the KJV are Deut. 23:17–18; 1 Kgs. 14:22–24; 15:12; 22:46; 2 Kgs. 23:7; Joel 3:3. The NT references in the NRSV are in 1 Cor. 6:9; and 1 Tim. 1:10. Myers and Scanzoni, *What God Has Joined Together?* 96, list thirteen different English translations of the two words since 1961.

32. Alice Ogden Bellis and Terry L. Hufford, *Science, Scripture, and Homosexuality* (Cleveland: Pilgrim Press, 2002), 110. Martin, "*Arsenokoites* and *Malakos*," 119–22.

33. Nissinen, *Homoeroticism*, 118.

34. Soards, *Scripture and Homosexuality*, 20.

35. See Thomas E. Schmidt, *Straight and Narrow: Compassion and Clarity in the Homosexuality Debate* (Downers Grove, IL: InterVarsity Press, 1995), 96–97.

36. Ibid., 97.

37. Seow, "Textual Orientation," 32n15.

38. Ibid., 22. C.-L. Seow notes that Jude, in the Greek text, indicates that the people of Sodom and Gomorrah have "practiced immorality in the same way [as the angels in Genesis 6] and pursued other flesh (*sarkos heteras*)." The flesh that the men of Sodom pursued was angelic, "other, different," the word from which we get "hetero," as in "heterosexual."

39. Blount, "Reading and Understanding," 34: "The worst thing is that they worship and serve not the Creator, but the creature. Their problem was idolatry."

40. Alan Brash, *Facing Our Differences: The Churches and Their Gay and Lesbian Members* (Geneva, Switzerland: WCC Publications, 1995), 44.

41. Nissinen, *Homoeroticism*, 105.

42. Ibid., 105.

43. Helminiak, *What the Bible Really Says*, 80.

44. Nissinen, *Homoeroticism*, 107.

45. See ibid., 104 for the Greek words.

46. Ibid., 107.

47. Ibid, 107. See, e.g., Robert A. J. Gagnon, *The Bible and Homosexual Practice: Texts and Hermeneutics* (Nashville: Abingdon Press, 2000), 364.

48. Nissinen, *Homoeroticism*, 107.

49. Ibid., 108.

50. Ibid.

51. Myers and Scanzoni, *What God Has Joined Together?* 98. They refer to John Boswell, *Christianity, Social Tolerance, and Homosexuality* (Chicago: University of Chicago Press, 1980), 158, 203–5.

52. See Robert Jewett, "The Social Context and Implications of Homoerotic References in Romans 1:24–27," in Balch, ed., *Homosexuality, Science, and the "Plain Sense" of Scripture*, 229–30.

53. David E. Fredrickson, "Natural and Unnatural Use in Romans 1:24–27: Paul and the Philosophical Critique of Eros," in Balch, ed., *Homosexuality, Science, and the "Plain Sense" of Scripture*, 204.

54. Ibid., 205.

55. Ibid., 216.

56. Jeffrey S. Siker, "Gentile Wheat and Homosexual Christians: New Testament Directions for the Heterosexual Church," in Brawley, ed., *Biblical Ethics and Homosexuality*, 143.

57. Ralph McInerny, "Are There Moral Truths That Everyone Knows?" in Edward B. McLean, ed., *Common Truths: New Perspectives on Natural Law* (Wilmington, DE: Intercollegiate Studies Institute, 2000), 1. The *New Catholic Encyclopedia* defines natural law as "a law or rule of action that is implicit in the very nature of things. . . . More properly, however, it is applied exclusively to man and proceeds from human nature as rational. . . . For St. Thomas Aquinas, 'natural law' is nothing other than the participation of eternal law in rational creatures." *New Catholic Encyclopedia* (New York: McGraw-Hill, 1967), vol. 10, s.v. "Natural Law." Charles E. Rice claims that "morality is governed by a law built into the nature of man and knowable by reason. Man can know, through the use of his reason, what is in accord with his nature and therefore good. . . . The natural law is therefore a rule of reason, promulgated by God in man's nature, whereby man can discern how he should act" (*50 Questions on the Natural Law: What It Is and Why We Need It* [San Francisco: Ignatius Press, 1999], 30, 31, and 51).

58. *Oxford English Dictionary* (*OED*), s.v. "Prejudice," offers these, among many, definitions of prejudice: "a judgment formed before due examination; a premature or hasty judgment; a prejudgment . . . a preconceived idea of what will happen."

59. Stephanie Rosenbloom, "Religious Leaders Clash on 'Meet the Press,'" *New York Times*, November 28, 2004, on nytimes.com, 11/28/04, pg. 2.

60. See Marlene Zuk, *Sexual Selections: What We Can and Can't Learn about Sex from Animals* (Berkeley: University of California Press, 2002), 176. The original source is Bruce Bagemihl, *Biological Exuberance: Animal Homosexuality and Natural Diversity* (New York: St. Martin's Press, 1999).

61. Gagnon, *The Bible and Homosexual Practice: Texts and Hermeneutics.*

62. Ibid., 488.

63. Ibid., 364.

64. Ibid., 157.

65. Ibid., 142.

66. Ibid., 391.

67. See Dan O. Via and Robert A. J. Gagnon, *Homosexuality and the Bible: Two Views* (Minneapolis: Augsburg Fortress, 2003), 103.

68. Nissinen, *Homoeroticism*, 120–21.

69. David G. Myers, excerpt from *Psychology*, 7th ed. (New York: Worth Publishers, 2004). Available at www.davidmyers.org

70. Via and Gagnon, *Homosexuality and the Bible*, 103.

71. Schmidt, *Straight and Narrow*, 155.

72. Andrew Comiskey, *Pursuing Sexual Wholeness: How Jesus Heals the Homosexual* (Lake Mary, FL: Creation House, 1989), 44.

73. Myers, excerpt from *Psychology*.

74. Gagnon, *The Bible and Homosexual Practice*, 254.

75. Ibid., 493.

76. Ibid., 470.

77. Hays, "Awaiting the Redemption," 8.

78. Ibid. Marion Soards also treats Romans 1 as relevant to contemporary Christian people who are homosexual. His rationale is much the same as that of Hays. Indeed, he agrees with Hays on the two criteria for condemning homosexual intercourse: It is a graphic example of human fallenness, and it rejects the created order of heterosexual marriage. See Soards, *Scripture and Homosexuality*, 21–23.

79. See, for example, the research of Hershberger, Levay, Allen and Gorski, Gladue, Mustanki and Bailey, and others, in Myers, excerpt from *Psychology*. Available at www.davidmyers.org.

80. Hays, "Awaiting the Redemption," 13.

81. Nor is there any cultural agreement on the nature of marriage. Stephanie Coontz in *Marriage, a History: From Obedience to Intimacy or How Love Conquered Marriage* (New York: Viking Penguin, 2005), 24, says, "So it ought to be easy to cut through all the historical and cultural differences to find marriage's common features and explain why the institution is so ubiquitous. But talk about opening a can of worms! . . . After a half a century there is still no definition everyone accepts."

82. Stanley J. Grenz, *Sexual Ethics: An Evangelical Perspective* (Louisville, KY: Westminster John Knox, 1997), 230.

83. Schmidt, *Straight and Narrow*, 39. Cf. Ulrich W. Mauser, "Creation and Human Sexuality in the New Testament," in Brawley, ed., *Biblical Ethics and Homosexuality*, 3–15.

84. Bird, "The Bible in Christian Ethical Deliberation," 167n55 [emphasis added].

85. Furnish, 'The Bible and Homosexuality," 22.

86. Ibid.

87. Ibid. Furnish notes, "The concern in these verses is much narrower: to explain why, ordinarily, a man is moved to leave his own blood kin to join himself in sexual union with a woman."

88. Ibid., 23.

89. David L. Balch, "Concluding Observations by the Editor," in *Homosexuality, Science, and the "Plain Sense" of Scripture*, 288.

90. Ibid.

91. See Coontz, *Marriage, a History*, 24.

92. Gagnon, in Via and Gagnon, *Homosexuality and the Bible*, 61.

93. Cited in Herman C. Waetjen, "Same-Sex Relations in Antiquity and Sexuality and Sexual Identity in Contemporary American Society," in Brawley, ed., *Biblical Ethics and Homosexuality*, 107–8.

94. The authors of the Confession of 1967 were not yet sensitive to the issue of women's rights. However, in the Kenyon Case in 1974, as we discussed in chap. 3, the Permanent Judicial Commission of the General Assembly affirmed that the equality of all people before God that the Confession of 1967 had applied to people of color was also applicable to women.

95. In June 1968, Barth's assistant, Eberhard Busch, drafted a letter under Barth's direction that constituted a partial, and only possible, retraction of his views on homosexuality. The letter was in response to a request that Barth join with others in protesting "defamation," and juridical "penalizing" of homosexuals who had committed no crime. Busch wrote, "Prof. Barth is today not completely satisfied any more with his former, incidental comments and would certainly formulate them today somewhat differently . . . he could, in conversation with doctors and psychologists, come to a new judgment and exposition of the phenomenon." However, Busch continued, "Naturally you would gladly hear that from him. But since he must allow all kinds of restrictions befall him as an over-82-year-old man, he does not now have the requisite time left for it. That time he thinks he ought to deploy, with the powers remaining to him, to the work on themes and tasks that seem to him more important." See Karl Barth, "Freedom for Community," in *Theology and Sexuality: Classical and Contemporary Readings*, ed. Eugene F. Rogers Jr. (Oxford, UK: Blackwell Publishers, 2002), 114–15.

96. Karl Barth, *Church Dogmatics*, III/4, *The Doctrine of Creation*, ed. G. W. Bromiley and T. F. Torrance (Edinburgh: T. & T. Clark, 1961), 163.

97. Elouise Renich Fraser, "Karl Barth's Doctrine of Humanity: A Reconstructive Exercise in Feminist Narrative Theology" (PhD diss., Vanderbilt University, 1986), 123n24: "The German phrase for both 'man and woman' as well as 'husband and wife' is *Mann und Frau*. . . . Barth's intention to use husband-wife as a paradigm for man-woman makes it difficult to determine which set of terms is more appropriate. In any case, it is not wrong to see husband-wife informing every reference to man-woman in this anthropological definition."

98. Fraser, "Barth's Doctrine of Humanity," 134. See Barth, *CD*, III/2:314.

99. Fraser, "Barth's Doctrine of Humanity," 203. See Barth, *CD*, III/2:290. To feel the full power of Barth's earlier rejection of any form of natural theology, see *Natural Theology: Comprising "Nature and Grace" by Professor Dr. Emil Brunner and the Reply "No" by Dr. Karl Barth*, trans. Peter Fraenkel, intro. John Baillie

(London: Geoffrey Bles: Centenary Press, 1946), 74. Barth declares that "the image of God in man is totally destroyed by sin. Every attempt to assert a general revelation has to be rejected. There is no grace of creation and preservation. There are no recognizable ordinances of preservation. There is no point of contact for the redeeming action of God. The new creation is in no sense the perfection of the old but rather the replacement of the old man by the new."

100. Fraser, "Barth's Doctrine of Humanity," 221–22. It is significant that here, exegetically, Barth moves away from Jesus and the Gospels, on which he based his definition of humanity, and uses instead Gen. 2 and the Pauline epistles, especially Eph. 5. Fraser notes that Barth appeals to Eph. 5 as the interpretive key to every Old and New Testament text on the relationship between man and woman. (Eastern Baptist Seminary was renamed Palmer Theological Seminary on July 1, 2005.)

101. Fraser, "Barth's Doctrine of Humanity," 217. See Barth, *CD,* III/4:166. Barth says, "The command of God shows him [a man] irrefutably—in clear contradiction to his own theories—that as a man he can only be genuinely human with woman, or as a woman with man. In proportion as he accepts this insight, homosexuality can have no place in his life, whether in its more refined or cruder forms."

102. Comiskey, *Pursuing Sexual Wholeness,* 40.

103. Jim Wallis, editor-in-chief of *Sojourners* magazine, said: "I can't ignore 3,000 verses in the Bible on poverty." See Leslie Scanlon, "'Monologue of the Religious Right' is over, Jim Wallis tells LPTS," *Presbyterian Outlook,* April 4, 2005, 4.

104. Luke Timothy Johnson, *Scripture and Discernment: Decision Making in the Church* (Nashville: Abingdon Press, 1996), 90, comments, "Luke has left his reader in no doubt concerning God's intention: From the beginning, God has willed the salvation of the Gentile world." See, 89–90, the many anticipations of Acts 10–15 in Luke and Acts. Johnson, 107, further comments, "The words of Jesus and the Scripture are normative for the believers, but in a way that allows new and deeper understanding of them."

105. Johnson, *Scripture and Discernment,* 147. Gagnon, in *Homosexuality and the Bible,* 43–44, fails to recognize the consistent biblical characterization of Gentiles as sinners, both in their being and in their behavior. Gagnon's rejection of the analogy of Gentile inclusion is further based on a series of false assumptions, such as the notion that homosexuality is a chosen condition. Thus he dismisses the analogy on grounds that are irrelevant.

106. Johnson, *Scripture and Discernment,* 147. See, further, 89–108 and 144–148.

107. Siker, "Gentile Wheat and Homosexual Christians," 146. For an expanded version of this testimony, see Jeffrey S. Siker, "Homosexual Christians, the Bible, and Gentile Inclusion: Confessions of a Repenting Heterosexist," in Jeffrey. S. Siker, ed., *Homosexuality in the Church,* esp. 187–90.

Chapter 6: Real People and Real Marriage

1. George Chauncey, *Why Marriage? The History Shaping Today's Debate over Gay Equality* (New York: Basic Books, 2004), 133: "One study had shown that of couples together for ten years, breakup rates were 4 percent for married heterosexual couples, 4 percent for gay men, and 6 percent for lesbians. Other comparative studies showed virtually no difference in the quality of relationships between gay couples and heterosexual couples."

2. David G. Myers and Letha Dawson Scanzoni, *What God Has Joined Together? A Christian Case for Gay Marriage* (San Francisco: HarperSanFrancisco, 2005), 68: "Regardless of the process, the consistency of the genetic, neural, and biochemical findings has swung the pendulum toward a greater appreciation of biological influences. If biology indeed proves critical (perhaps especially so in certain environments), such would explain why we do not experience our own sexual orientation as a choice."

3. Chauncey, *Why Marriage?* 153: "The belief that homosexuality is a sinful choice instead of a minority status is especially pronounced among people with a fundamentalist or evangelical worldview."

4. Ibid., 152: "A major Pew Foundation study conducted in early 2004 found that a person's belief or disbelief in the mutability of homosexual identity was a more powerful predictor of their attitudes toward gay people than education, knowing someone gay, or 'general ideological beliefs.'"

5. Paul in 1 Cor. 7:9: "If they are not practicing self-control, they should marry. For it is better to marry than to be aflame with passion." John Calvin, *Institutes of the Christian Religion* 2.8.41: "The companionship of marriage has been ordained as a necessary remedy to keep us from plunging into unbridled lust."

6. Heinrich Bullinger, writing in the Second Helvetic Confession (1566), commends those "who have the gift of celibacy from heaven," but wisely says, "But if, again, the gift be taken away, and they feel a continual burning, let them call to mind the words of the apostle: 'It is better to marry than to be aflame' (I Cor. 7:9)" (*Book of Confessions*, 5.245).

7. See "Bishops Seek Easier Dismissal of Priests," *Los Angeles Times*, Nov. 18, 1993. The story also cites "Jason Berry, who has written a book on the issue, estimated that the [R.C.] church spent $400 million from 1984 to 1992 to settle cases involving 400 priests."

8. A May 1991 survey of fifty presbyteries of the Presbyterian Church (U.S.A.) revealed that there were sixty-four ongoing or recent sexual misconduct cases reported, most involving ministers engaging in sexual intercourse outside of marriage. See "Policy and Amendments Aim to Combat Sexual Misconduct," *Presbyterian Outlook*, January 6–13, 1992, 6.

9. Westminster Confession of Faith, chapter 24, 3 in *The Confession of Faith of the Assembly of Divines at Westminster, From the Original Manuscript Written by Cornelius Burges in 1646*, ed. S.W. Carruthers (n.p,: Presbyterian Church of England, 1946).

10. *Minutes*, PCUSA, 1930, 87.

11. Jack Rogers, *Reading the Bible and the Confessions: The Presbyterian Way* (Louisville, KY: Geneva Press, 1999), 82 and 84.

12. "Three Gay Couples Argue for Right to Marry," *USA Today*, November 19, 1998, 7A.

13. Chauncey, *Why Marriage?* 62–63.

14. Stephanie Coontz, *Marriage, a History: From Obedience to Intimacy or How Love Conquered Marriage* (New York: Viking Penguin, 2005), 186, "In the thirteenth century the English jurist Henry de Bracton declared that a married couple is one person, and that person is the husband. When Lord William Blackstone codified English common law in 1765, he reaffirmed this principle. . . . This doctrine of coverture, in which the legal identity of a wife was subsumed ('covered') by that of her husband, was passed on to the colonies and became the basis of American law for the next 150 years." Cf. 115 and 194.

15. *Minutes*, PCUSA, 1930, 79–82.

16. Benton Johnson, "From Old to New Agendas: Presbyterians and Social Issues in the Twentieth Century," in *The Confessional Mosaic: Presbyterians and Twentieth-Century Theology*, ed. Milton J Coalter, John M. Mulder, and Louis Weeks (Louisville, KY: Westminster John Knox, 1990), 220.

17. CNN.com, November 18, 1998. "Three Gay Couples," 7A. Chauncey, *Why Marriage?* 131, notes that in a friend-of-the-court brief in the Massachusetts case "neither the ability nor willingness to procreate has ever been a condition for entering a marriage, nor has the inability to have children been a legal basis for ending a marriage. Statutory law and case law both showed that marriage instead established certain relational rights and obligations, which were designed to 'support individuals' expectations of emotional and sexual intimacy, vows of fidelity and commitment and sharing of economic assets and support.'"

18. Christopher Calhoun, Public Policy Advocate, L.A. Gay and Lesbian Center, in a letter to the *Los Angeles Times*, July 24, 1999, B7.

19. Chauncey, *Why Marriage?* 86.

20. "The particular form taken by modern heterosexism is largely derived from sexism." Dale B. Martin, "*Arsenokoites* and *Malakos*: Meanings and Consequences," in Robert L. Brawley, ed., *Biblical Ethics and Homosexuality: Listening to Scripture* (Louisville, KY: Westminster John Knox, 1996), 129.

21. Chauncey, *Why Marriage?* 147.

22. Anna Quindlen, "Now Available: Middle Ground," *Newsweek*, July 11, 2005, 74. Commenting on resistance to the "morning-after pill," to prevent pregnancy, Quindlen states, "The rise and righteous indignation of the powerful religious right have been fueled by the transformation of women's lives. . . . If easy access to a pill that has been shown to significantly decrease the number of abortions is not a welcome development, what is the real point of the anti-abortion exercise? Is it to safeguard life, or to safeguard an outdated status quo in which biology was destiny and motherhood was an obligation, not an avocation? America

leads the industrialized world in its abortion rate. Perhaps that is because it leads in hypocrisy as well."

23. Jerry Falwell, *Listen America!* (New York: Bantam Books, 1981), 159.

24. Cited in Chauncey, *Why Marriage?* 148.

25. Dobson first came to wide public notice while teaching child development at the University of Southern California with his book *Dare to Discipline*, which encourages parents to spank their children with "sufficient magnitude to cause the child to cry genuinely." See James Dobson, *Dare to Discipline* (Wheaton, IL: Tyndale House Publishers, 1970), 35.

26. Dan Gilgoff, "An Evangelical Leader Steps Squarely into the Political Ring," *U.S. News & World Report*, January 16, 2005, 62.

27. *U.S. News & World Report*, January 17, 2005, 69.

28. David Van Biema, "The Twenty-five Most Influential Evangelicals in America," *Time*, February 7, 2005, 36.

29. Dr. James Dobson, *Focus on the Family Newsletter*, April 2004 (mailed to more than 2,000,000 people). Cited in Jeff Lutes, *A False Focus on My Family* (Lynchburg, VA: Soulforce, 2005), 6.

30. Focus on the Family, CitizenLink, *Q&A: The Homosexual Agenda*, July 25, 2003. Cited in Lutes, *A False Focus*, 6.

31. "The Battle for Marriage," television simulcast to more than 700 churches, May 23, 2004. Cited in Lutes, *A False Focus*, 6.

32. See Susan Olasky, "Femme Fatale," *World* 12, no. 2 (March 29, 1997): cover story. Cf. J. Lee Grady, "EPA Panel Rebukes *World*," *Christianity Today*, August 11, 1997, 58.

33. James C. Dobson, "Spooked by the Zeitgeist: Don't Give In to Feminist Pressure to Rewrite the Scriptures," *World* 12, no. 7 (May 3, 1997).

34. Doug Le Blanc, with Steve Rabey, "Bible Translators Deny Gender Agenda," *Christianity Today*, July 14, 1997, 62–63.

35. "Conservative Christians' Outcry Forces Cancellation of New Bible," *Los Angeles Times*, May 31, 1997, B4. *World* 12, no. 10 (June 14, 1997) ran a story headlined "Bailing Out of the Stealth Bible." In fact, Zondervan continued its translation work and in 2005 produced the TNIV, or Today's New International Version, in contemporary English, using gender-inclusive language. Moderate evangelicals praised the translation while Dobson and the more extreme fundamentalists remained relatively quiet. See "New Bible Woos Young Adults, Skirts Critics," in *Christian Century*, March 8, 2005, 14–15.

36. Aída Besançon Spencer, "Power Play," *Christian Century*, July 2–9, 1997, 618–19.

37. Ibid.

38. Michael G. Maudlin, "Inside CT," *Christianity Today* 41, vol. 8 (July 14, 1997): 4.

39. Dobson, "Spooked by the Zeitgeist."

40. Cited in Martin E. Marty, "Doing It by the Book," *Christian Century*, May 3, 2005, 47.

41. Family.org: A Web site of Focus on the Family. http://www.family.org/welcome/bios/A0022947.cfm.

42. Focus on the Family joined with the following groups in sponsoring a full page advertisement in *USA Today* to support their assertion that "Freedom from homosexuality *is possible*": National Association for Research and Therapy of Homosexuality; Exodus International, North America; Parents and Friends of Ex-Gays; Evergreen International; Transforming Congregations; International Healing Foundation; JONAH (Jews Offering New Alternatives to Homosexuality); and New Life Clinics.

43. James Dobson, *Bringing Up Boys*, "The Origins of Homosexuality," 115, cited in Lutes, *A False Focus*, 4. See the American Psychiatric Association, *Position Statement on Homosexuality*, 2000: "The APA affirms its 1973 position that homosexuality per se is not a diagnosable mental disorder. Recent publicized efforts to re-pathologize homosexuality by claming that it can be cured are often guided not by rigorous scientific or psychiatric research, but sometimes by religious and political forces opposed to full civil rights for gay men and lesbians."

44. H. Newton Malony, "Changes in Attitudes toward Homosexuality among Mental Health Professionals: What Pastoral Counselors Need to Know," in *Pastoral Care and Counseling in Sexual Diversity*, ed. H. Newton Malony (New York: Haworth Press, 2001), 24.

45. For further discussion, see: "Gay and Lesbian Issues: Background and Ordering Information," http://www.psych.org/public_info/homose-1.cfm

46. American Psychological Association Statement on Homosexuality, July 1994.

47. Dr. Joseph Nicolosi, Focus on the Family's "Love Won Out" conference, Oklahoma City, 2003, cited in Lutes, *A False Focus*, 4.

48. Ibid.

49. David G. Myers, excerpt from *Psychology*, 7th ed. (New York: Worth Publishers, 2004). Available at www.davidmyers.org, p. 2.

50. American Psychoanalytic Association, "Position Statement on the Treatment of Homosexual Patients," http://www.apsa.org/pubinfo/homosexuality.htm.

51. American Anthropological Association, "Statement on Marriage and the Family," http://www.aaanet.org/press/ma_stmt_marriage.htm.

52. Cited in Lutes, *A False Focus*, 7.

53. Joseph Nicolosi, *Reparative Therapy of Male Homosexuality* (Northvale, NJ: Jason Aronson, 1991). Freud is the most-cited author in the book. See Myers and Scanzoni, *What God Has Joined Together?* 72–73 for further background.

54. Nicolosi, "Love Won Out," 2003, cited in Lutes, *A False Focus*, 10.

55. Nicolosi, "Love Won Out," Focus on the Family Web site, cited in Lutes, *A False Focus*, 10. The American Psychiatric Association, *Position on Therapies Focused on Attempts to Change Sexual Orientation (Reparative or Conversion Therapies)*, approved by the assembly May 2000, states, "The American Psychiatric Association opposes any psychiatric treatment, such as 'reparative' or conversion therapy, which is based upon the assumption that homosexuality per se is a mental disorder

or based upon the a priori assumption that a patent should change his/her sexual homosexual orientation."

56. Policy Statement: "Homosexuality and Adolescence," American Academy of Pediatrics, 1993, http://www.clgs.org/5/_6_1.html.

57. See the American Psychiatric Association, *Position on Therapies*, cited in Lutes, *A False Focus*, 11.

58. "Just the Facts about Sexual Orientation and Youth: A Primer for Principals, Educators, and School Personnel," APA ONLINE (American Psychological Association, Public Interest Directorate), http://www.apa.org/pi/lgbc/publications/justthefacts.html.

59. Gil Alexander-Moegerle, *James Dobson's War on America* (Amherst, NY: Prometheus Books, 1997).

60. Nicolosi, Focus on the Family's "Love Won Out" conference, cited in Lutes, *A False Focus*, 12.

61. *Straight Answers, Exposing the Myths and Facts about Homosexuality*, Focus on the Family's *Love Won Out* series, p. 12, cited in Lutes, *A False Focus,* 12.

62. People for the American Way, "Right Wing Watch Online," November 12, 1999: "November: Attacks on Science, Homosexuality, and the APA," http:///www.pfaw.org/pfaw/general/default.aspx?oid=3546.

63. See Jack B. Rogers and Donald K. McKim, *The Authority and Interpretation of the Bible: An Historical Approach* (San Francisco: Harper & Row, 1979), 296–97.

64. Focus on the Family, *Citizen* magazine, January 2003. Cited in Lutes, *A False Focus*, 8. In another context, Dr. Maier, spokesperson for Focus on the Family, in an interview with Pete Winn said, "I think, as believers we always have to differentiate between that homosexual individual—whom God loves too dearly and who is made in His image—and the gay activist movement, which I believe is a tool of Satan" (*The Unhappy Truth about Being Gay*, Focus on the Family's *Citizenlink*, July 16, 2004).

65. Cited by David Batstone, "Jimmy Swaggart Tells Congregation He'd Kill Gays," 09.22.2004 http://www.sojo.net.

66. Chris Hedges, "Soldiers of Christ II: Feeling the Hate with the National Religious Broadcasters," *Harper's Magazine*, May 2005, 57. Frank Wright, the new president of the NRB, said, "We will fight the Fairness Doctrine, tooth and nail. It could be the end of Christian broadcasting as we know it, if we do not."

67. Coretta Scott King, in a speech at the Palmer Hilton Hotel, quoted in the *Chicago Defender*, April 1, 1998. Cited in Lutes, *A False Focus*, 13.

68. Lewis B. Smedes, "Exploring the Morality of Homosexuality," in *Homosexuality and Christian Faith: Questions of Conscience for the Churches*, ed. Walter Wink (Minneapolis: Fortress Press, 1999), 77.

69. Barbara Kantrowitz, "State of Our Unions," *Newsweek*, March 1, 2004, 44. Cf. Coontz, *Marriage, a History*, 274.

70. *National and International Religion Report* 9, no. 9 (April 17, 1995): 8. Cf. Don S. Browning, Ronnie J. Miller-McLemore, Pamela D. Couture, K. Brynolf

Lyon, Robert M. Franklin, *From Culture Wars to Common Ground: Religion and the American Family Debate* (Louisville, KY: Westminster John Knox, 1997), 52.

71. Leon Eisenberg, "Is the Family Obsolete?" *Key Reporter* 60, no. 3 (Spring 1995): 3. Cf. Browning et al., *From Culture Wars to Common Ground*, 52.

72. Browning et al., *From Culture Wars to Common Ground*, 53–54.

73. Sharon Jayson, "Divorce Drops, Along with Marriage," *USA TODAY*, July 18, 2005, notes that "divorce is on the decline in the USA, but a report to be released today suggests that may be due more to an increase in people living together than to more lasting marriages."

74. Cited in Ronald J. Sider, "The Scandal of the Evangelical Conscience," *Books & Culture*, January/February 2005, 9 and 39.

75. Cheryl Wetzstein, "Who's Happier Ever After?" *Insight* 14, no. 36 (September 28, 1998): 38, cited in *Current Thoughts and Trends*, March 1999, 13.

76. Browning et al., *From Culture Wars to Common Ground*, 3 and 53.

77. Chauncey, *Why Marriage?* 34. "The movement to come out was also profoundly shaped by the sexual revolution. . . . All around them, they [homosexuals] saw their heterosexual friends decisively rejecting the moral codes of their parent's generation, which had limited sex to marriage, and forging a new moral code that linked sex to love and common consent."

78. This material was provided by the Lambda Legal Defense and Education Fund to Ontario Consultants on Religious Tolerance Web site. I downloaded it on February 16, 2005.

79. Cited in Sider, *Books & Culture*, 9.

80. Ibid.

81. Pam Belluck, "To Avoid Divorce, Move to Massachusetts," November 14, 2004, www.nytimes.com/2004/11/14/weekinreview, printed November 17, 2004, p. 1.

82. Ernest Trice Thompson, *Presbyterians in the South*, vol. 2, *1861–1890* (Richmond: John Knox Press, 1973), 218.

83. Ronald W. Hogeland, "Charles Hodge, the Association of Gentlemen and Ornamental Womanhood: 1825–1855," *Journal of Presbyterian History* 53, no. 3 (Fall 1975): 248.

84. Chauncey, *Why Marriage?* 137. He cites *New York Times*, March 12, 2004, A12.

85. Chauncey, *Why Marriage?* 140: "In Massachusetts, two-thirds of the 752 couples to get marriage licenses on the first day were lesbian, and 40 percent of those couples had children living with them. This shouldn't be surprising, since having children raised the stakes for everyone."

86. "Bush Seeks Constitutional Ban on Same-Sex Marriage," *Los Angeles Times*, February 25, 2004, A1.

87. Cass R. Sunstein, "President Versus Precedent," *Los Angeles Times*, February 26, 2004, B13.

88. "The Politics of Gay Marriage," *Los Angeles Times*, February 26, 2004, B12.

89. Chauncey, *Why Marriage?* 133.

90. Chauncey, *Why Marriage?* 133: "In 1995, after conducting a comprehensive review of research studies, the American Psychological Association concluded that 'not a single study has found children of gay or lesbian parents to be disadvantaged in any significant respect relative to children of heterosexual parents.' But they were disadvantaged, the brief commented, by the fact 'that the State will not allow their parents to marry.'" [See note 27, American Psychological Association, *Lesbian and Gay Parenting: A Resource for Psychologists* (Washington, DC: APA, 1995).]

91. "Gays and the Gospel: An Interview with Troy Perry," *Christian Century,* September 25–October 2, 1996, 896.

92. Mel White, *Stranger at the Gate: To Be Gay and Christian in America* (New York: Simon & Schuster, 1994).

93. Soulforce, www.soulforce.org.

94. At the time of this writing, same-sex marriage was legal in the Netherlands, Belgium, Spain, and Canada.

95. Lewis Smedes, "Like the Wideness of the Sea," *Perspectives,* May 1999, 12.

Chapter 7: Recommendations
for the Presbyterian Church (U.S.A.)

1. Timothy C. Morgan, "Racist No More? Black Leaders Ask," *Christianity Today,* August 13, 1995, 53.

2. *Minutes, 213th General Assembly, 2001, Part I, Journal* (Louisville, KY: Office of the General Assembly, 2001), Comment, p. 61, on Commissioners' Resolution 01-3, p. 487. "That the 213th General Assembly (2001) 1. Confesses the corporate guilt the Presbyterian Church (U.S.A.) shares for the evils of slavery and requests forgiveness from God and from all God's children whose lives have been damaged by these sins."

3. The General Assembly of the United Presbyterian Church in the U.S.A. gave definitive guidance against the ordination of "self-affirming, practicing" homosexuals. At the same time, the policy adopted called on United Presbyterians "to reject in their own lives, and challenge in others, the sin of homophobia," which was defined as "the irrational fear of and contempt for homosexual persons." For the larger context, see *Minutes,* UPCUSA, 1978b, 61–62 and 261–67.

4. "Confessional Nature of the Church Report," *Minutes,* PC(USA), 1986, Part I, 29.116.

5. Ibid.

6. A contemporary example would be a revision of the Southern Baptist Convention's "Faith and Message" (BFM) statement in 2000, which stated that "the office of pastor is limited to men as qualified by Scripture." On October 20, 2000, former President Jimmy Carter severed his lifelong connection with the Southern Baptist Convention in a letter that deplored the denomination's "increasingly rigid

creed." Carter used as an example the denomination's declaration in May 2000 that women should no longer be called as senior pastors. The current convention stance left no room for individual interpretation of Scripture, Carter stated, and instead exalted the interpretations of the convention's leadership ahead of "Jesus Christ, through his words, deeds, and personal inspiration, as the ultimate interpreter of the Holy Scriptures" (Larry Stammer, "Carter Cuts Ties to Baptist Convention and Its 'Rigid' Conservatism," *Los Angeles Times*, October 21, 2000, A13).

7. *Book of Confessions*, 6.175.

8. This flaw was based on erroneous interpretations of both the Bible and the *Book of Confessions*.

9. *Book of Order*, G-2.0100.

10. Ibid.

11. *BO*, G-2.0300.

12. *BO*, G-2.0400.

13. *BO*, G-2.0500.

14. I have dealt with this in my book *Reading the Bible and the Confessions: The Presbyterian Way* (Louisville, KY: Geneva Press, 1999).

15. *BC*, 7.234–7.242.

16. *BC*, 10.3, lines 30–32.

17. *BC*, 8.11.

18. *BC*, 8.26 [emphasis added].

19. *BC*, 9.44.

20. *BC*, 4.087 [emphasis added].

21. Professor Bos then alerted her colleague at Louisville Presbyterian Theological Seminary, Christopher Elwood, professor of historical theology. Together, they proposed a change back to the original text to the General Assembly but without success.

22. *The Heidelberg Catechism* (New York: United Church Press, 1962).

23. *DOCTRINAE CHRISTIANAE COMPENDIVM: seu COMMENTARII CATECHETICI*, ex ore D. ZACHARIAE VRSINI, vere Theologi. LONDINI: Excudebat Henricus Midoletonus impensis Thomae Chardi, 1586.

24. *Catechismus, oder Kurzer Unterricht Christlicher Lehre, wie derselbe in denen Reformirten Kirchen und Schulen in Deutschland wie auch in America, getrieben wird.* Philadelphia: Gedruckt und zu haben bey Steiner und Kaemmerer, 1795.

25. *Het Boeck Der Psalmen.* Middelbvrgh: Richard Schilders, druker der Staten s' landts van Zeelandt, 1591.

26. *THE SUMME OF CHRISTIAN RELIGION DELIVERED BY ZACHARIAS URSINUS First, by way of CATECHISM, and then afterwards more enlarged by a sound and judicious EXPOSITION, and APPLICATION of the same. First Englished by D. HENRY PARRY, and now again conferred with the best and last Latine Edition of D. DAVID PAREUS, sometime Professor of Divinity in Heidelberge.* LONDON, Printed by James Young, and are to be sold by Steven Bowtell, at the signe of the Bible in Popes-head Alley. 1645. This commentary on

the catechism by its primary author was translated into English in editions published in England in 1587, 1591, 1611, 1617, 1633, and the one cited in 1645. These would surely have been known to the Westminster divines, since they desired to be in harmony with the other Reformed churches.

27. *The Heidelbergh Catechism Or Method of Instruction IN THE CHRISTIAN RELIGION As The same is taught in the Reformed Churches and Schools of Holland and Germany. Translated for the Use of the Reformed Protestant Dutch Church, of the City of New-York, and other Schools in America.* New-York, Printed: PHILADEL-PHIA, Re-printed by ANTHONY ARMBRUSTER, in Race-Street, between Second and Third-Street, near the Sign of the Green Tree, 1765.

28. The translators used the NEB only for 1 Cor. 6:9–10. For the other three texts related to Answer 87, they used the Revised Standard Version.

29. *The New English Bible: New Testament* (New York: Oxford University Press, 1961, 2nd ed., 1970).

30. *The Holy Bible, containing the Old and New Testaments with the Apocryphal/Deuterocanonical Books*, New Revised Standard Version (New York: Oxford University Press, 1989). For the Revised Standard Version and a sample commentary, see Markus Barth, *Ephesians*, vol. 2, Anchor Bible (Garden City, NY: Doubleday, 1974).

31. *The Greek New Testament: being the text translated in the New English Bible, 1961*, edited with introduction, textual notes, and appendix by R. V. G. Tasker (London: Oxford University Press, 1964).

32. Henry George Liddell and Robert Scott, *A Greek-English Lexicon* (Oxford: Clarendon Press, 9th ed., 1940, with a revised supplement, 1996).

33. *The Bible and Holy Scriptures Conteyned in the Olde and Newe Testament* (Geneva: Printed by Rovland Hall, 1560).

34. *Book of Order*, G-5.0103.

35. *BO*, G-3.0401.

36. *BO*, G-4.0403.

37. *BO*, G-6.0106a.

38. *General Assembly News* vol. 1996, no. 3 (July 2, 1996): 1.

39. The same assembly, on the same day, voted to authorize the stated clerk to explore entering a friend-of-the-court brief in favor of the civil rights of same-sex couples. The assembly also voted to approve a budget that eliminated the only paid staff person supporting marriage and family life ministries. The assembly sent its prohibition of homosexual ordination for the vote of the 172 presbyteries as Amendment B.

40. James D. Anderson, "The Lesbian and Gay Liberation Movement in the Presbyterian Church (U.S.A.), 1974–1996," *Journal of Homosexuality* 34, no. 2 (1997): 57.

41. "'Fidelity and Chastity' Amendment Debate Clouded by Imprecise Definitions," *News Briefs*, December 13, 1996, 3–5.

42. The word "sodomy" is not a biblical word, as I have shown in chapter 5. It was used to describe sexual acts not open to procreation and as such applied to heterosexual as well as homosexual behavior.

43. Westminster Confession of Faith, chapter 24, 3 in *The Confession of Faith of the Assembly of Divines at Westminster, From the Original Manuscript Written by Cornelius Burges in 1646*, edited by S. W. Carruthers (n.p.: Presbyterian Church of England, 1946).

44. *BC*, 6.145, note concerning 1647 edition.

45. *BC*, 5.247.

46. *BC*, 7.061; cf. *BC*, 7.229.

47. *BC*, 7.249.

48. Ibid.

49. *BC*, 7.219.

50. *BC*, 5.217.

51. *BC*, 6.114.

52. I tried to remedy this problem in my book *Presbyterian Creeds: A Guide to the Book of Confessions* (Louisville, KY: Westminster John Knox Press, 1991).

53. Correspondence and personal discussion with Fred Beuttler. See his article "Making Theology Matter: Power, Polity, and the Theological Debate over Homosexual Ordination in the Presbyterian Church (U.S.A.)," *Review of Religious Research* 41 (1999): 239–61.

Index